# Quilts
## of the
# GOLDEN WEST

### MINING THE HISTORY OF THE GOLD AND SILVER RUSH

#### BY CINDY BRICK

# QUILTS of the GOLDEN WEST

## MINING THE HISTORY OF THE GOLD AND SILVER RUSH

### BY CINDY BRICK

EDITOR: DEB ROWDEN

DESIGNER: BRIAN GRUBB

PHOTOGRAPHY: AARON T. LEIMKUEHLER,
MELLISA KARLIN MAHONEY

ILLUSTRATION: LON ERIC CRAVEN

TECHNICAL EDITOR: DEB McCURNIN

PRODUCTION ASSISTANCE: JO ANN GROVES

*Unless otherwise noted, photos and other illustrations are from the author's collection. All quilt photos by Mellisa Karlin Mahoney.*

PUBLISHED BY:
Kansas City Star Books
1729 Grand Blvd.
Kansas City, Missouri, USA 64108

First edition, first printing
ISBN: 978-1-935362-14-2

Library of Congress Control Number: 2009931850

Printed in the United States of America by Walsworth Publishing Co., Marceline, MO

To order copies, call StarInfo at (816) 234-4636 and say "Books."

 KANSAS CITY STAR QUILTS
*Continuing the Tradition*

PickleDish.com
The Quilter's Home Page

www.PickleDish.com

# ACKNOWLEDGEMENTS

Much of the writing for this book took place not long after a traumatic event in our lives: the death of my dad, after more than three years fighting multiple melanoma. After his funeral, I was exhausted. Even the smallest things took twice as long to accomplish. Writer's block? I had "Writer's Fog." My grateful thanks to those who came alongside during this difficult time to help and encourage…bring us meals; listen to tears and frustration; bear with long, involved stories about the Forty-Niners, mining, lost treasures, the Girls (and equally long arguments about quilt names)…and just cut me some slack. Much love and dazed thanks goes to my courageous mom, Bonnie DeVries, who spent many long hours sewing and pressing, along with Aunt Corrinn, friend Anne and cousin Dawn. My darling girlies, Jess and Angel; siblings Mike and Lori; friends Chris, Jo and Constance, along with cousins Phil, Joanie and Krindi – love you, too, guys. Finally, special thanks to my editor Deb Rowden, who "ooched" and pushed and encouraged me along the way.

Additional thanks go to Mellisa Mahoney, the photographer whose fine work documents all of the quilts in this book; the staff at the Road to California conference, where the "California Gold" exhibit came to life; Jan Magee of *Quilter's Newsletter*; and the staff at the Rocky Mountain Quilt Museum, especially the director, Brenda Ohlschwager and Karen Roxburgh, the Collections Manager. Their willingness to share the museum's quilts, and their interest in the "California Gold" exhibit, gave this book wings. (Thank you also to RMQM's previous director, Paula Pahl, whose thoughtful interest started the process.) Jeananne Wright, Kathy Litwinow, Janice Fisher, Suzanne Swenson and Kim Wuhlfert cheerfully loaned quilts for months on end, and listened to this girl yammer on about California Gold. (Let me know when I can return the favor.) Jo Morton and Andover Fabrics donated fat quarters from her latest line. Many thanks!

The staff at the Kansas City Star's books division lent their magic to this title. They were the ones who saw a book in the "California Gold" article, and without knowing about the publishing credits already under my belt, asked if I would do this one, too.
Thank you to each and every one of you.

## About the Author

Cindy Brick has worn several hats during her career, including teacher, writer, editor, designer…and just plain quilter. A former editor at *Quilter's Newsletter*, she also has been a columnist for *McCall's Quilting*; a managing editor for several newsletters, including the *Quilt Heritage Foundation*; and an editor for several books. Cindy has written hundreds of articles for newspapers and magazines, and is the author of the *Fabric Dating Kit*, *Quilts of the Great Depression*; *The Stitcher's Language of Flowers*; *Hanky Panky Crazy Quilts*; and the historical/how-to study *Crazy Quilts*.

Cindy is a professional judge, a nationally-known teacher, and an American Quilter's Society-certified appraiser. She's appeared in television and online specials, including an HGTV quilt history special, *Simply Quilts* and *The Quilt Show*. She lives and works in Castle Rock, Colorado with her husband and two crazed Weimaraners. Visit Cindy at the Brickworks website: *www.cindybrick.com*.

### Dedication

*For Peter and Bonnilou DeVries.*
*Without your love and encouragement,*
*I would be… well, I wouldn't.*

*And to David – always, my darling.*

# QUILTS OF THE GOLDEN WEST
## Mining the History of the Gold and Silver Rush

A Daughter of the West

Pioneer era quilts are some of America's most-treasured antiques.
Is it the wonderful combination of shade and color, the many different prints? Perhaps it's the many unusual patterns, each representing an idea or event. Or do we just admire the workmanship achieved under less-than-ideal conditions?

Late nineteenth-century quilters admired their emigrant forebears no less than we do. They carefully preserved their ancestors' quilts, and sometimes, like us, made copies of older quilts, so they would be preserved. But these quilters also, like us, made commemorative quilts to honor those same pioneers.

One of their favorite commemorative fabrics appeared in the 1880s: a peachy-golden shade some today call "butterscotch" or "caramel." This warm-toned shade featured a number of small-scale prints, from dots to squiggles, and was mixed into the scrap combinations so popular in the last quarter of the 19th century. A little of this soft gold also gave a glow to planned quilts in pieced and appliquéd patterns, especially star and floral designs.

Decades had gone by since various gold and silver rushes had occurred. Old-time emigrants were beginning to look back nostalgically on their long travel overland or oversea to get to the mining camps...and what it was like in the camps themselves. The easily mined gold was largely gone, except for a token nugget on a watch chain, necklace or brooch. But the Forty-Niners, as well as those before and after them, could still well remember the effort it took to collect those bright pieces of metal.

Survivors of the Gold Rush period, many of them now aging and in poor health, published a number of first-hand accounts, preserved so their children and grandchildren would better understand. Anniversary celebrations were held to honor the Gold Rush. Magazines like *Harper's Bazaar* made special trips to the country's gold, silver and other mineral camps, to talk to older participants. And Americans, who often celebrated their favorite times and memories in their quilts, nicknamed these brand-new peachy-toned fabrics California Gold.

## Come visit the period.

Placer Mining and the Discovery of Gold in the Black Hills in „75".

"Gold is the most exquisite of all things. Whoever possesses gold can acquire all that he desires in the world. Truly, for gold he can gain entrance for his soul into Paradise."

— *Christopher Columbus*
*Treasure: Lost, Found and Undiscovered*

# PREFACE

Ever since man (and women!) have admired a shining bracelet, purchased a house, or bought groceries, precious metals have played an important part in our lives – and finances. Gold and silver started as a basis not only for jewelry and a mode of exchange, but entire economies. Other metals, including copper, also played a factor. They could be obtained in return for a service or item – but best of all, they could be obtained directly from the land. If you weren't rich, the possibility (however faint) still existed – a few days... or months... or years... digging in the right place, and you'd be rich!

Over the centuries, people have had plenty to say about these precious metals – how they were used and valued, what they could be exchanged for. And those changing values could literally destroy – or make – a millionaire in just a few years.

Opinions on the subject have been expressed in a variety of ways, mostly in print by male writers and politicians. But others also held strong views, even if they weren't generally allowed to vote, and few held public office (at least before the constitutional amendment on voting was ratified in 1920). Women subtly made their opinions on gold, silver and other precious metals – money and finances in general – in their journals, the political parties and historical events they participated in... and, surprisingly, in their needlework – even their quilts.

Pioneer era quilts are some of America's most-treasured antiques. Is it the wonderful combination of shade and color, the many different prints? Perhaps it's the many unusual patterns, each representing an idea or event. Or do we just admire the workmanship achieved under less-than-ideal conditions?

Late nineteenth-century quilters admired their emigrant forebears no less than we do. They carefully preserved their ancestors' quilts, and sometimes, like us, made copies of older quilts, so they would be preserved. But these quilters also, like us, made commemorative quilts to commemorate an event, celebrate a visit... or express an opinion.

In the 1880s, a warm peachy-golden fabric appeared, in a color some today call "butterscotch" or "caramel." This warm-toned shade featured a number of small-scale prints, from dots to squiggles. It was used for clothing and quilts, especially the latter's scrap quilt combinations so popular in the last quarter of the 19th century. A little of this soft gold also gave a glow to planned quilts in pieced and appliquéd patterns, especially star and floral designs.

It had a nostalgic name, celebrating the emigrants and miners known as Forty-Niners, who made their way to California ("The Golden State"). The fabric's popular title?

**California Gold.**

Decades had gone by since the first gold discoveries of the Forty-Niners. Old-time emigrants were beginning to look back nostalgically on their long travel overland or oversea to get to the mining camps... and what it was like in the camps themselves. The gold was largely gone, except for a token nugget on a watch chain, necklace or brooch. But the Forty-Niners, as well as those before and after them, could still well remember the effort it took to collect those bright pieces of metal.

Survivors of the Gold Rush period, many of them now aging and in poor health, published a number of first-hand accounts, preserved so their children and grandchildren would better understand. Anniversary celebrations were held to honor the Gold Rush. Magazines like *Harper's Bazaar* made special trips to the country's gold, silver and other mineral camps, to talk to older participants. And Americans, who often celebrated their favorite times and memories in their quilts, added a touch of California Gold to their fabric mix.

But how did this period come about?

*The Depression Era jump-started interest in mining, first for survival, then as the decades rolled on, for tourism. These postcards are typical examples for c.1930-60.*

# CHAPTER 1

# A CLOSER LOOK AT CALIFORNIA'S GOLD RUSH

Of all the events in America's storied history, the California Gold Rush is one of its most homegrown. Unlike the Revolution, it had nothing to do with countries in Europe. It was not organized, at least at by large corporations or political groups. And financially, it not only changed individuals' lives, but als made a young and struggling country very, very rich. What's amazing is that it all started by accident

# How It Started

If it weren't for a little flash of light, James Marshall would have never noticed. He was busy – his boss, John Sutter, had hired him to start a sawmill near Culluma (now known as Coloma, near Sacramento), and there was plenty to do. Marshall and his hired men, along with ten Indians, built the mill on the American River, and dug a mill race, for the water to run through and provide the power needed. But it wasn't quite deep enough yet... Every night, they opened the gate to let the water through to scour out the ditch. And every morning, Marshall checked on the mill race's progress.

Sometime between January 18 and 20, 1848, the sun glinted on something bright six inches under the water:

> "I was entirely alone at the time," Marshall later remembered. "I picked up one or two pieces and examined them attentively; and having some general knowledge of minerals, I could not call to mind more than two which in any way resembled this – *sulphuret of iron*, very bright and brittle; and *gold*, bright, yet malleable; I then tried it between two rocks, and found that it could be beaten into a different shape, but not broken. I then collected four or five pieces and went up to Mr. Scott (who was working at the carpenters bench making the mill wheel) with the pieces in my hand and said, 'I have found it.'
>
> 'What is it?' inquired Scott.
>
> 'Gold,' I answered.
>
> 'Oh! no,' returned Scott, 'that can't be.'
>
> I replied positively, – 'I know it to be nothing else.'"
>
> *(www.malakoff.com/marshall.htm)*

No one in the group of men that gathered around was positive the bright pieces were gold – they'd never seen any in its natural state. Jenny Wimmer, the cook and laundress, was cooking a fresh batch of soap: "'This is gold, and I will throw it into my lye kettle... and if it is gold, it will be gold when it comes out.' I finished off my soap that day and set it off to cool, and it stayed there till next morning... A plank was brought for me to lay my soap onto, and I cut it into chunks, but it was not be found. At the bottom of the pot was a double handful of potash, which I lifted into my hands, and there was my gold as bright as could be." (from *They Saw the Elephant*, see Sources on page 128)

The gold nuggets Marshall picked up that day eventually disappeared. (They were used to pay for groceries later that year.) But the excitement they produced was contagious. Within a month, Marshall's employees were too busy panning for gold to go to work; one recorded gathering up a hundred dollars in a week... a fortune in those days.

Marshall's employer, John Sutter, was hoping his colony would keep on growing. It had survived California's Bear Flag Revolt a little more than a year before. Californians tried to start their own republic; they were rescued from the Mexican army by the U.S., which promptly annexed the area instead. Sutter, who had gotten a land grant, didn't really care who was in charge, as long as he could continue to raise cattle and build. He tried to keep the gold discovery quiet by asking his men to say nothing. And for a while, it worked. But chance comments from one of Sutter's hired men started a rush.

Sutter was in real trouble. People swarmed over his land to pan for gold. They shot his cattle and wrecked crops that hadn't already spoiled from lack of harvest. He had no employees to run them off – the men had quit to go look for gold themselves. Sutter's little fiefdom was gradually crumbling... all because his manager found some bright bits of metal on that warm January day.

# How It Spread

The excitement for gold was contagious. People who had come to farm suddenly changed their minds, and headed toward the gold diggings, instead. Whole ships were left stuck in San Francisco's harbor, their cargoes mildewed and rotting, their crews deserted. Merchants, who stocked the pans and gear and dry goods these new miners needed, suddenly made fortunes. Restaurants, hotels and even laundries sprang up to feed and care for the population flooding in from California, Oregon and nearby states.

The Gold Rush might have remained a regional event. Without it, California was a young and raw state, separated from the rest of the country by a series of mountain ranges and deserts. Nearby states only had small populations, and the same travel problems. Ship's berths were expensive and time-consuming. Transportation meant a long, slow trip in any case, with no guarantee of making it intact. Why come all that way just for farmland and cattle, even if it was good land?

But things were changing in the rest of the country:

The Oregon Trail was guiding pioneers west... and more than a few were beginning to take the cutoff that led to California. Other trails were beginning to be more heavily used. Civilization had crossed the Missouri river, and was gradually moving west. The Preemption Act of 1841 allowed squatters to eventually claim the land they lived and worked on. That, and the Homestead Act of 1862 that eventually supplanted it, meant that a man could buy or prove up on acres and acres of land. Land to keep, or expand on.

There was unrest back east. Regular financial crises, or "panics," drained off bank accounts and bankrupted business. (See Chapter 2 for more.) Although the Panic of 1837, a financial crisis that kept the U.S. banks from redeeming in silver or gold, had eased somewhat, work was still hard to find. Why not move west, and start in a new community?

Mining experience was available – and ready. Although gold had been found in streams and elsewhere since the founding of Jamestown, VA, centuries earlier, America's first bona fide gold rush was in Georgia, beginning in 1829. But after decades of production, the gold veins there were beginning to play out. Experienced miners began looking for other opportunities.

And the final, deciding factor, one that could make anyone rich, and forever change their lives:

# GOLD.

Sutter might still have succeeded in keeping the news hush-hush, if it had not been for Samuel Brannan, a San Francisco merchant who set up a store near Sutter's Fort. Brannan also published a newspaper: the *California Star*. He saw the gold used by Sutter's employees to pay for

their groceries and other sundries, and a brilliant plan ensued. Brannan quickly beefed up his store, and planned to set up others. (It is said that he purchased every shovel in San Francisco.) Then he deliberately ran through the streets of San Francisco, a vial of gold in his hand, shouting "Gold! Gold from the American River!" Within a year, his Sutter's Fort store alone was doing $150,000 a month in sales. Samuel Brannan had become California's first millionaire, without picking up a grain of gold dust.

Brannan took special care to spread the word further east, as well. His *California Star* printed every little detail, and eventually other newspapers further picked up the news. It took a while. In late August of 1848, the *New York Herald* was the first big newspaper on the East Coast to mention the gold camps. Other newspapers took up the buzz and on December 5, President James Polk confirmed the richness of the gold strikes in an address to Congress. A messenger reached Washington, D.C., two days later, carrying proof of Polk's words: 230 ounces of California gold, packed in a tea caddy.

Many decided to head west, but the first news of the gold rush reached the East in the fall – with the winter soon to come. Better to wait, most people decided. Go in the spring, when the weather was better and traveling easier. Besides, grass and water would be available to keep the horses and oxen going. So California's biggest influx of emigrants was the year *after* Marshall's accidental discovery: 1849. These hardy souls became the **Forty-Niners.**

# How They Got There

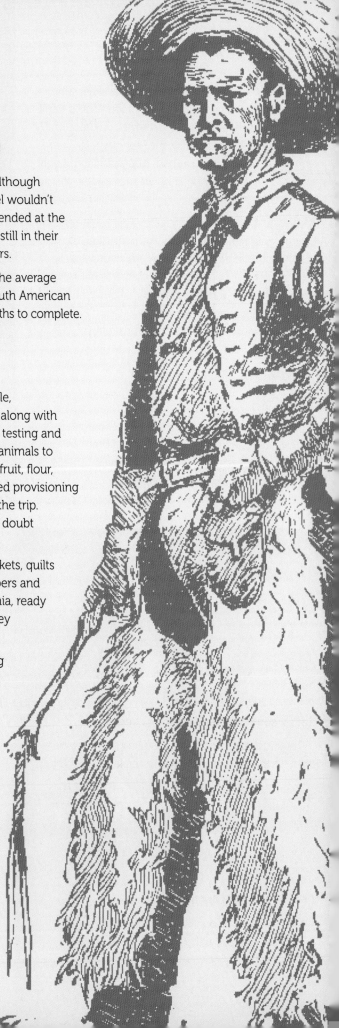

Traveling by train or stagecoach was possible – to a point. Although Congress had passed a railroad act, transcontinental train travel wouldn't be complete until 1869 – 20 years later. Most organized travel ended at the Missouri River. Western towns like Kansas City or Denver were still in their infancy, though growing quickly from the new influx of travelers.

Passage to California usually came via one of two ways for the average Forty-Niner: either via the Isthmus of Panama or round the South American Horn by ship, or overland by wagon train. Either route took months to complete.

## One If By Land...

The first supply needed was a good guidebook. One 1849 title, Joseph Ware's *Emigrant's Guide to California,* even promised, along with information on routes, altitude and weather, "full directions for testing and assaying gold and other ores." Next was a sturdy wagon, with animals to draw it. And finally, months' worth of supplies, including dried fruit, flour, coffee, beans, bacon and salt pork. (Many guidebooks suggested provisioning at jumping-off points, instead of carrying food at the onset of the trip. Merchants at river towns like St. Joseph and Independence no doubt agreed... and raised their prices accordingly.)

Precious possessions were carefully packed, along with blankets, quilts and tents. But these preparations were often hurried. Newspapers and other accounts suggested that the gold lay in heaps in California, ready to pick up. What if someone else got your share? Luzena Stanley Wilson caught the fever, though it was tempered somewhat:

"The gold excitement spread like wildfire, even out to our log cabin in the prairie, and as we had almost nothing to lose, and we might gain a fortune, we early caught the fever. My husband grew enthusiastic and wanted to start immediately, but I would not be left behind. I thought where he could go I could, and where I went I could take my two little toddling babies. Mother-like, my first thought was of my children. I little realized then the task I had undertaken. If I had, I think I should still be in my log cabin in Missouri. But when we talked it all over, it sounded like such a small task to go out to California, and once there fortune, of course, would come to us.

"It was the work of but a few days to collect our forces for the march into the new country, and we never

# Pioneers prospecting in the far West.

gave a thought to selling our section [sp], but left it, with two years' labor, for the next comer. Monday we were to be off. Saturday we looked over our belongings, and threw aside what was not absolutely necessary. Beds we must have, and something to eat. It was a strange but comprehensive load which we stowed away in our "prairie-schooner", and some things which I thought necessities when we started became burdensome luxuries…"

*Luzena Stanley Wilson, 1881 Memoir*

Wagons often traveled in companies – a wise, though slower decision, when more than a few individual wagons were decimated by sickness, accidents or Indian attacks. At least there were others to help guard the train, including animals, nurse the sick, bury the dead, and repair the inevitable breakdowns. Guides could be hired to get the group through; their standard price was $1 a head. Most often, the route used the new California Trail, which took advantage of routes already established on the Oregon and Mormon Trails, but then branched down via Utah, Wyoming or Utah eventually to the Humboldt Valley, so animals could get the grass and water they needed. The route meant enduring hellish spots like Death Valley and hauling wagons through the Sierra Nevada Mountains before the towns and gold fields of western California were finally achieved. All sorts of variations were possible. (Another route took travelers even further south into Mexico, across Veracruz.)

The cross-country trip took nearly two months – and often longer than that. It risked disease (though the 1849 season was much less than other years), the inevitable accidents, Indian attack and theft, and dealing with poor weather and water conditions. Emigrants were forced to lighten the same possessions they'd packed so carefully, to help their wagons – and animals – keep going. One family history recounted:

"After the loss of three of Grandfather Reynolds' horses – from drinking alkali water, and grass very scarce – it was necessary to lighten the wagons, and the following was left by the

13

*Ocean Waves, c.1885. Perhaps its maker added California Gold patches in honor of her long voyage to the goldfields decades before. Collection of Suzanne Swenson.*

## Or Two If By Sea

Many *Argonauts*, as Gold Rush pioneers were called, preferred traveling to the gold fields by sea, especially the thousands who came from other countries. The choices generally boiled down to two options:

*Sail south and around the tip of South America, a trip that took 5-8 months and covered approx. 18,000 nautical miles. Deal with poor food and the dangers of traveling so far south, where storms were common. Or:

*Sail down the Atlantic side of the country to the Isthmus of Panama. Disembark, pack up possessions, then ship them (and yourself) by mule and canoe over the narrow neck of Panama, a trip that could take weeks through the jungle, and often exposed its travelers to malaria and fever. Once through, wait for a ship on the Pacific side that was bound for San Francisco or other places north. This trip may have been shorter, but it no less dangerous.

By the mid-1850s, paddle-wheeled steamers made the trip on both sides of the Atlantic, including reputable vessels like the *SS Central America* (more on her later). These expeditions, like those overland, held their share of dangers, but also a chance to view unusual sights and places for the adventurous.

The rigors of travel, worries about children or the farm, as well as limited finances, kept many women home. But some insisted on accompanying their men, whether husbands or brothers. A very few traveled alone or with other women.

roadside with Grandmother's tears: five good quilts, handmade; one feather bed; extra cooking utensils; a keg of syrup; one gun, broken up so the Indians couldn't use it; and one wagon with the sign on it 'help yourself' in hopes the next train would get it."
*(Ho for California)*

Unless they were ill or giving birth, women did not generally ride in the wagons – they walked. So did their children. There were always the chores of breaking camp in the morning, then repeating the process at night. After cooking and cleaning, there was always mending or repairs to take care of, children to watch. The schedule was grueling, to say the least... assuming, that is, that your party safely made the trip.

Nevertheless, more than 25,000 emigrants traveled across the continent for California. The next year, 1850, saw nearly double that amount.

"Made on the way" Gold Rush quilts: various family histories have labeled an elaborate pieced or appliquéd quilt as being stitched while its maker made the long trip West. The idea is a romantic one, but unrealistic. How could anyone have much time to piece or appliqué, given the many hours needed to keep the wagon going, animals and people fed... not to mention the scarcity and expense of tools (needles and pins were hand-stamped, and much more harder to obtain) and fabrics... and available time?

Imagine yourself stitching by the light of a smoky campfire, or trying to keep your balance on a heaving ship's deck – and the answer is clear. Some stitching might have been possible in a simple pattern for a quilt top. (Some quilts of this type do exist.) Quilts could have been started. But most probably, these pieces were largely stitched (and definitely quilted) *after* the maker had arrived at her destination.

# We're Here. Now What?

That was undoubtedly the question on many a person's mind when they disembarked at the San Francisco wharf, or finally rumbled into town, dusty and tired. The sleepy little town that held barely 1,000 inhabitants in 1848 roared into a 25,000 population by 1850. The harbors were still full of empty ships, deserted by their crews. (Many were eventually sunk and used for landfill.) Other ships brought in fancy merchandise and supplies destined for the newly-rich claim owners at the western mining camps. Nearly anything, from picks and gold pans, to linen and lace, was available – provided you had the funds to pay.

Fine restaurants and gambling houses, hotels and brothels lined the streets, along with businesses. Some people stayed in town for some weeks to re-supply… but most were too impatient. They headed for the gold camps for another hot and dusty trip.

Few women were able to accompany their men to the goldfields… but for those who did, the first order of business was invariably finding somewhere to stay. A cabin was luxury; the order of business more often tents, sometimes with wooden floors. Families even continued to bed down in the wagons that had brought them west, like Mrs. John Berry, who arrived with her husband and children in October 1849:

"The rains set in early in November, and continued with little interruption until the latter part of March and here were we poor souls living almost out of doors. Sometimes I would come out of a wagon (that is & has been our bedroom since we left the States) & find the tent blown down the shed under which I cooked blown over & my utensils lying in all directions, fire out & it pouring down as tho the clouds had burst… amid all the war of the elements feel a consolation in thinking I had all my family about me." *(They Saw the Elephant)*

The more resourceful women contrived to make money off the basics: a good meal, a comfortable (or at least bug-free) bed, clean clothes. Many miners had left their families behind, and were desperate for the basics of home living. One of Luzena Smith's first acts was to sell biscuits for a $10 gold piece (see Sources on page 128). Mary Jane Caples switched to pie:

"I concluded to make some pies and see if I could sell them to the miners for their lunches, as there were about one hundred men on the creek, doing their own cooking - there were plenty of dried apples and dried pealed peaches from Chili, pressed in the shape of a cheese, to be had, so I bought fat salt pork and made lard, and my venture was a success. I sold fruit pies for one dollar and a quarter a piece, and mince pies for one dollar and fifty cents. I sometimes made and sold, a hundred in a day, and not even a stove to bake them in, but had two small dutch ovens."…..

*—Goldrush.com*

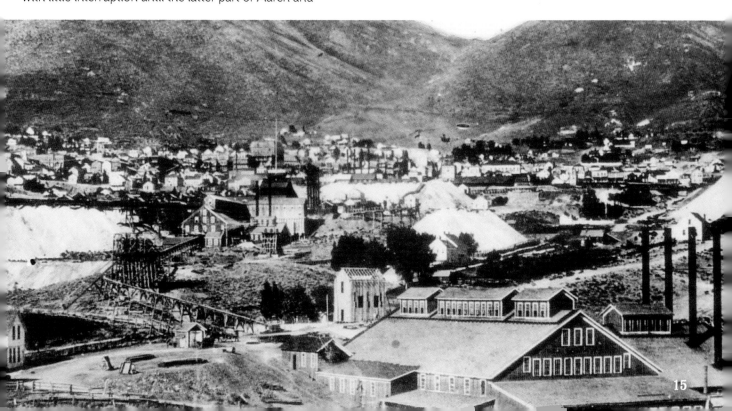

Other women washed clothes and mended. For miners who were making a good living at their claims, and willing to send their dirty laundry as far as San Francisco – or even China! – a dollar or more per shirt was nothing. (This was at a time when a dollar a day in gold dust was considered a good wage, if washed out on the claim.) If industrious, a woman could make as much as her male counterpart on the claim – or even more.

*Californos,* the native Mexicans of the state, did the same jobs as the white women who had come into camp – but got little respect. The other Native women of the state received similar treatment, as did many of the nationalities that emigrated, especially the Chinese.

And finally there were the entertainers and "good-time" girls, who kept their patrons busy measuring out gold dust for their favors. The lawless nature of many of the gold camps helped these women gather as much as they could haul in – provided, of course, they didn't spend it themselves on gambling, alcohol or drugs.

There was one other option, one that a few hardy women like Nellie Cashman and Marie Pantalon took: they worked claims along-side the men, panning or sluicing out the gold themselves (see *Girls of the Golden West*, pages 76 and 70).

# Mining Methods

Early reports made it sound as if gold could be scooped up off the ground in the early camps. Some early miners did just that, making the equivalent of six years' work in as many months. But it depended on the claim. Others made a few dollars every day...or nothing. Generally gold was either *panned* or *sluiced* from *placers* – deposits of nuggets (large grains) or dust (small grains) that had collected on the bottoms of streams or rivers. These were often *alluvial,* i.e., a good distance away from the mother lode they had originally eroded from. The miner's goal was to clean out the placer (taken from the Spanish word *placera,* or "alluvial sand") – and find that elusive mother lode.

First, a claim had to be established. This was the miner's property, but only as long as he or she was actively working on it. Many people 'sampled' claims, moving on quickly from anything they considered lower grade. Louise Clapp pointed out:

"They [the miners] are always longing for 'big strikes.' If a 'claim' is paying them a steady income, by which, if they pleased, they could lay up more in a month than they could accumulate in a year at home, still they are dissatisfied, and in most cases, will wander off in search of better 'diggings.' There are hundreds now pursuing this foolish course, who, if they had stopped where they first 'camped,' would now have been rich men."          – *A Mine of Her Own*

The next step was to extract the gold, as we silver and other minerals that clung to it. Panning the gold was the most basic method. Gr was placed in a special pan with grooves, wat added, then the whole shaken and rinsed unt the heavier gold remained in the bottom. This method demands patience, and often gave w to the more efficient sluice mining, where ore was shoveled into a *sluice* box with riffles at t bottom to catch the gold as the water washe over it. (*Rockers* or *cradles,* which shifted bac and forth, were also used.) Sluice boxes were easier to maintain with partners who took tur shoveling ore and adjusting the sluice. Both methods involved standing in cold rushing st water all day, producing sickness and arthritis

Long Toms were a favorite of California mi these boxes were 6-12 feet long, with a scr set at an angle on one end, and a short sluice the other. They worked on the same principle sluice box, but did not have to be shifted back forth, like a rocker.

**H**ydraulic mining came into common use by 1853, using large nozzle hoses to sluice through gravel and silt, changing the stream bed in the process and sending large quantities of silt downstream. "Hydraulicking" was so destructive that flushing debris into streams was finally banned in 1884. *Dredges* also came into use.

And finally, miners collected ore by *hard rock mining*, digging the mineral out of veins in the rock, using outcroppings, and then tunnels. This method was used for more permanent *lode mining* by companies, and still produces most of the gold, silver, copper and other mineral mining today. Sodium cyanide and zinc were mixed with finely-ground ore, then sulfuric acid added to produce a sludge that could be further melted down and purified, then poured into bars or slugs for further processing later on.

## The Gold Rush Slows

The number of people "rushing" to California slowed to a trickle by 1855. Hard rock and hydraulic mining were still cost-effective, but done by large companies, rather than individuals. Many miners had no intention of staying in California, anyway. They made their fortune (and/or lost it), and returned home, or they died from sickness or accidents, or they were killed during a bar fight or robbery. Much of the surface mineral was collected. And what a collection it was! An estimated $6.6 billion was collected just by hydraulicking alone.

But other changes were more far-reaching. An estimated 300,000 people had poured into California during the Gold Rush: approximately half by land, and half by sea. San Francisco's population was approximately 150,000, and California's size, after her admission to the Union in 1850, made her the 31st state. Mining was still important, but one of several varied occupations, thanks in part to the ranchers and merchants who made a tidy profit on the many emigrants who poured in. California's access to the rest of the world was assured, thanks to technological advances funded by gold. More ships plied a regular route to the state, and the railroad was coming.

Some people made a comfortable living for their hard work – but many others spent their money as fast as they could make it, or lost it all. The *Old Settler's Song*, one of the popular tunes of the period, explained it well:

"I've traveled all over this country
Prospecting and digging for gold
I've tunneled, hydraulicked and cradled
And I have been frequently sold.

For each man who got rich by mining
Perceiving that hundreds grew poor
I made up my mind to try farming
The only pursuit that was sure."

The Gold Rush was over. Many of the California miners were leaving… to follow the next Gold Rush. Only this time, it was in Colorado.

**T**hree miles west of Plattsmouth, NE, is a field that was the traditional stopping place for miners headed to California's and Colorado's digging fields – as well as headed east after they went bust. Plattsmouth was one of the last places to stock up; local merchants told men, 'A month out there, and you can come back with a fortune.' It was just the thing greenhorns wanted to hear… unfortunately, most only made about $3 a day at their work, if that.

In 1859, a group of disillusioned miners decided to teach the merchants a lesson, and sack Plattsmouth. The townspeople had been tipped off; when the mob reached the edge of town, armed men were waiting for them. The miners were pushed to the edge of the Missouri river and told, "Swim to Iowa and don't come back." They had no choice, and plunged in – leaving guns, horses, weapons and gear behind. Those items promptly appropriated by the good people of Plattsmouth. The miners may also have buried small caches of valuables at the field, as well – money that may still be there.

—America's Lost Treasures

# RUSHES – AND PANICS

# CHAPTER 2

By 1852, two years after it entered the Union, California was no longer a quiet backwater. The state's non-Indian population was 250,000 – in other words, more than one percent of the nation's total population had managed to move to California in just four years! Two years earlier, there were 624 miners for every thousand people, but many realized they could do even better by supplying the miners' needs.

The Gold Rush ensured plenty of gold to meet those needs. From 1792-1847, total U.S. gold production was about 37 tons. California's output in 1849 alone exceeded this figure – and annual production from 1848-1857 averaged 76 tons. By 1860, California's gold production equaled more than $550 million – in 1860 values.

Then a series of events occurred, in quick succession. Emigration to California slowed to a trickle, as mining production declined and costs of living increased. Wages increased, driven in part by higher labor costs at the gold camps. Then in early fall of 1857, the sidewheel steamer *SS Central America* picked up its usual load of passengers on the eastern side of Panama, fresh from their ride on Cornelius Vanderbilt's new railroad across the Isthmus.

The *Central America* was considered one of the West's safest modes of transportation; it had already carried east a third of California's gold output, approximately $150 million. This trip was different. By late evening September 11, 426 of the 578 passengers and crew were lost in a huge hurricane that sank the ship after more than three days and nights of struggle, and the ocean floor was littered with more than three tons of gold bars, coins, nuggets and dust. The actual figure was much higher; many passengers did not declare their own money belts or carpetbags of cash, jewelry and diamonds. Nor could the survivors bring them on the rescue boats – the gold was simply too heavy.

Eastern banks had been counting on the Central America's gold to meet payrolls, and when it did not arrive, they began closing, along with stores and factories. The Panic of 1857 paralyzed the country and eventually spread to Europe – all because a steamer went down in a storm off North Carolina's Outer Banks.

ELKS CLUB - LEADVILLE, COLO. THIS IS THE HISTORIC TABOR OP...

Amazingly, the *Central America* was locate in 1986 in 8500 feet of water off Cape Hatter North Carolina. Much of the gold was salvag including bars of California gold and coins fr private mints that were practically unheard of… and in mint condition. The largest bar – 80-pound gold ingot poured by San Francisc assayers Kellogg and Humbert, was auctione in 2001 for $8 million, making it the most valuable currency in the world. Its 1857 valu $17,433.57. (For more information, see *Ship c Gold in the Deep Blue Sea* in Sources, page 1.

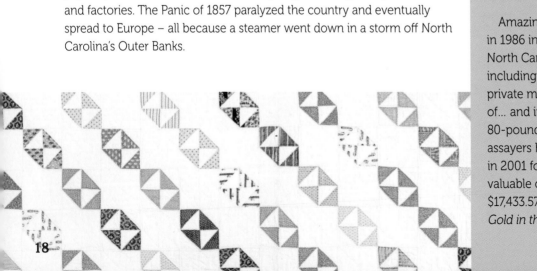

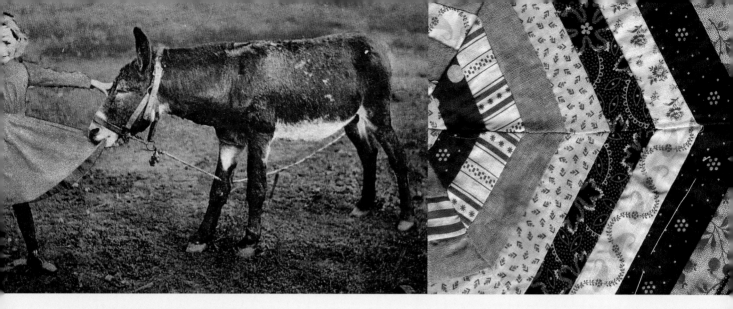

## Colorado Joins the Rush

Another **Gold Rush** saved the day – this time in Colorado. A group of Cherokee had noticed gold in the streams near Denver, but didn't stop – they were on their way to the gold fields. They did tell William Russell, who was married to a Cherokee woman, about their discovery. In February 1859, Russell persuaded his two brothers, along with several others, to stop and investigate on their way home from California. Though most of the party gave up and headed for home, Russell's party eventually panned out hundreds of dollars of gold from a small stream pocket near current-day Englewood, CO, not far from the new settlement of Denver, founded only the year before. They spread the word – and when larger amounts were found in Idaho Springs and elsewhere in the mountains, the Rush was on.

These pioneers called themselves the **Fifty-Niners**, and took as their motto "Pike's Peak or Bust!" (Major discoveries were made many miles from the actual mountain, though the 1891 **Cripple Creek** got quite close.) As in California, when placer mining gradually cleaned out gold dust and nuggets from the streams, miners turned to lode or *hardrock mining*, using wood framing to shore them up, and pumping systems to keep them free of water, a persistent problem in the Rockies.

Again, a small but hardy percentage of women accompanied men up into the mountains, including Augusta Tabor, Horace Tabor's first wife, and the first woman to venture into the California Gulch area near present-day Central City. Augusta became the camp's laundress, managed the post office, and served as the bank president when she weighed the men's gold on the scales she and Horace had brought with them. Horace helped out a little and prospected a lot, but the little gold he found could not be easily separated from the heavy black sand around it. The claim he developed was jumped – by the same man who'd suggested the Tabors winter in Denver that year!

After following the same pattern in various mining camps for the next decade – Augusta running the post office and general store, Horace achieving a modest success with mining – the couple struck it rich in Leadville, where two miners Horace staked to supplies discovered a rich mine. (Baby Doe and infamy followed. See page 56 for more.) But Horace made his biggest money in silver – the sticky black sand of years before was actually rich in silver ore.

Although silver had been discovered about the same time as gold deposits (the two minerals were often found together, in the company of copper or sulfides), it was worth very little, compared to gold. That changed when the U.S. Congress authorized large-scale purchases of silver for coinage purposes in 1878, reversing the **Panic of 1873**, which began when silver was set aside in favor of gold as the monetary standard. The resulting **Silver Boom** endured through the 1880s, and made many Coloradoans, including Horace and Augusta Tabor, rich.

Denver grew into a large city, fueled not only by gold, but the railroad, farming and cattle ranches. Smaller gold supply towns like Golden and Central City gained their share of prosperity, as well. Once again, a Gold Rush had worked its magic. The state that joined the Union in 1876 (before that, it was part of Kansas Territory) looked very different from the mountains and plains visited only by traders, Indian tribes and buffalo herds.

# Other Rushes

Colorado wasn't the only place to benefit from experience learned in the California gold fields. Other Western states, including Idaho, Montana, New Mexico and Arizona, experienced gold and silver rushes, the discoveries often made by miners on their way home from California. Nevada was especially blessed. The amazingly rich Comstock Silver Lode was discovered in 1857 near Virginia City, NV, then appropriated by a drifter, Henry Comstock, who cheated the original claim owners out of their discovery. Other Nevada mining camps carried a flourishing amount of miners, many who realized that their Irish forbears did not limit opportunities to succeed, like they had in towns like Boston and New York City. The Irish miners were particularly fond of Gaelic-themed dances like jigs, and loved a good song – a tendency entertainers like Lotta Crabtree were quick to cultivate.
(See more on Lotta in page 62.)

*Harper's Weekly visited Colorado miners in 1880, inspiring these drawings.*

**COPPER MINING ALSO FLOURISHED,** thanks in part to large deposits found in Arizona and Montana, among other states. The Anaconda Copper Mining Company was one of the largest, with mines, smelters and processing centers for shipping the ore out through the railroad. (The mine endured until 1947, after producing 94,900 tons of copper. Another mine of the same name, but in Arizona, produced 360 million tons of material during the 25 years it was operated.) Bisbee, AZ was also known for its heavy concentrations of copper ore, with silver ore included in the mix. Not all miners took ore from the claims they found; some, like Ferminia Sarras, preferred to sell them to others for development. (See more on Ferminia on page 68.)

Mining camps, whether they produced gold, silver or copper, were often short-lived, but produced heavily while they lasted. Businesses, gambling and entertainment houses followed the camps, moving on when profits dwindled. Silver prices stayed high, fueled by 1878's Bland-Allison Act, as well as 1890's Sherman Silver Purchase Act, which also required the government to purchase millions of ounces of native silver.

The West may have pumped tons of precious metals into the United States' economy, shoring up workers' wages and farm products prices. But the situation would be changing – soon.

Placer Mining and the Discovery of Gold in Black Hills in „75".

# CHAPTER 3:

# GOLD VERSUS SILVER: THE FIGHT FOR A STANDARD

Since time immemorial, gold and silver have been used as a currency standard. Many countries began their monetary systems by using one or both as the standard: any paper currency issued had its value set by the amount of precious metal it could be converted into.

The United States first based its system on the silver standard, using the Spanish milled dollar as a starting point. The first coins were minted via the Coinage Act of 1792; since Philadelphia was then the national capitol, it also became the site of the first mint. Money transactions could be made in many different ways, including foreign coins, as well as paper notes from the Massachusetts Bay Colony, beginning in the 1690s, and *colonial scrip* from each of the thirteen colonies in the early 1700s. A number of banks were issued *charters* to print their own currency, basing it (supposedly) on the gold and silver they held in reserve to redeem that paper money. Counterfeit notes were epidemic; banknotes from Ohio Territory banks became so notorious for problems, due to lax policing, that Ohio banks all became suspect. (see *A Nation of Counterfeiters* in Sources) Other notes, like the Dixie, were more reliable.

Soon after Louisiana became a part of the United States, a New Orleans bank issued bilingual ten-dollar bills, identified on one side by the French *dix*, or "ten." The bills came to be known as *dixies*. Eventually the term was applied to New Orleans. Daniel Decatur Emmett's song *I Wish I Was in Dixie*, written in 1859, expanded the term to all of the South... and eventually the Confederacy.

—*Dictionary of Misinformation*

*Above, a Californo vaquero, or cowboy*
*Below, a typical California gold rusher's*
*cabin, 1848*

Banknotes from the First Bank of the United States (1789-1811), and The Second Bank of the United States (1816-36) were validated directly by the U.S. Congress. But the first printing of banknotes, or greenbacks (named for the color on their back sides) weren't issued by the U.S. Government until 1862; they could not be directly exchanged for gold, but they could be used to buy gold certificate notes (printed first in 1882) that could.

California's Gold Rush directly challenged this system – and its reliance on Eastern business interests. The volume of gold was so high that for years, California was literally digging its own money. Eventually, the U.S. opened the San Francisco Mint in 1854 to serve California's gold mines; by the first year, it had turned $4 million of gold bullion into coins.

A third mint eventually began operating in Denver, CO as Clark, Gruber and Company in 1858, processing gold from the Pikes Peak Gold Rush into coins and gold bars. It was purchased by the U.S. Government in 1863, but then processed only gold bars, using Colorado ore from lode mining, which often contained silver, as well as gold. By 1859, at least $5.9 million in silver and gold was deposited yearly at the Mint, but silver and gold coins weren't minted there until 1906.

For many years, *bimetallism*, or both gold and silver, were accepted as a standard for currency, but it was an uneasy peace. Eastern business interests, and the banks connected with them, preferred gold because it was more readily accepted by other countries, especially European ones – and could therefore be more easily moved in and out of the system.

Even though they had access to gold, Western and "interior" (i.e., Midwestern) states tended to prefer silver; they had easy access to it, and being less expensive, silver could be easily used to pay wages and suppliers. Farmers felt that the silver standard kept prices for their products higher.

Western producers, being heavily invested in silver, would pressure their political interests to introduce legislation to buy silver bullion for coining. This kept silver in demand, but it also contributed to the financial instability in Panics. Banks would refuse to redeem their paper currency in either gold or silver, Eastern business interests would start shuttling their stock of gold bullion out of the country... and more instability would occur.

Several presidential campaigns in the latter part of the 19th century and beginning 20th centuries, took the fight for a gold or silver standard as their battle cry – financial conglomerates in the Northeast, or *gold bugs*, versus Western miners and Midwestern farmers, or *silverites*. Gold insect-shaped pins and motifs were popular ways to express one's affiliation; silver items, on the other hand, suggested the opposite.

The issue came to a head after Grover Cleveland's election as president in 1892. The Panic of 1893 was in full steam, fueled primarily by overbuilding and speculation in railroading – but then banks began failing, causing a run on the gold supply. Cleveland acted to repeal the 1890 Sherman Silver Act, causing silver prices to plummet, but preserving the gold standard. Many silver millionaires, like Horace Tabor, were ruined. Others, like Margaret Brown's husband J.J., had their income based on gold mines, so survived relatively unscathed. (See Molly's story on page 58 for more on the Browns.)

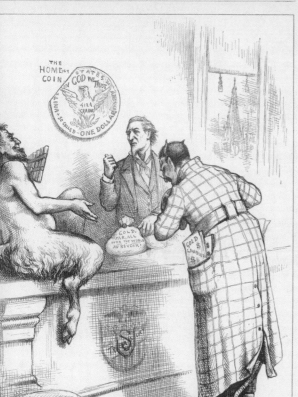

*The threat in this 1884 political cartoon from Harper's Weekly is clear: if Uncle Sam refuses to outlaw silver, plenty of gold is going to get sent overseas, instead. "Uncle Sam, in God you trust, but you will have to pay this gentleman if you don't repeal that bland silver act."*

The country was saved – but Western and interior interests paid the price.

The issue came to a head during the 1896 presidential election, when William Jennings Bryan, a lawyer and wildly popular public speaker, took his Free Silver platform to campaign against William McKinley, a former governor of Ohio, who favored high tariffs on goods, and the gold standard. "You shall not crucify mankind on a cross of gold," thundered Bryan at the 1896 Democratic convention (held in Denver, naturally).

For Bryan's Populist (eventually combined with Democratic) supporters, silver was a cheaper way to pay their debts, and would eventually restore them to prosperity while it kept the dollar from deflation. For McKinley's Republican supporters, such an act would send the country spinning back into inflation – and another Panic. Few people could discuss the subject peacefully. The campaign was filled with posturing and hyperbole, and even formerly innocent items, like the gold chrysanthemum (taken up by the Gold Standard people as their symbol) became hated. (Rose Wilder Lane's novel *Old Home Town* mentions one innocent family that is nearly run out of their Missouri town, all because they keep golden chrysanthemums in their yard.)

Quiltmakers, like the rest of the country, longed to register their strong opinions about gold and silver standards. Many rural quilters were Free Silver, and could have chosen a unique way to express it: their scrap quilts would contain a wide variety of colors and shades, but only one bright, prominently-placed gold patch. This one spot of gold marked them as Silverites. Both gold and silver standard proponents also freely displayed and used their candidate's face and mottoes on ribbons, handkerchiefs, banners and yardage, which they then stitched into scrap quilts and Crazy quilts.

William Jennings Bryan lost the election – and with it, any hope that the Sherman Silver act, would be reinstated. Bryan's loss in the 1900 election cemented the blow. Although the United States continued to keep repositories of both gold and silver, in Fort Knox as well as West Point, the Silver Standard was never again taken as seriously.

That didn't stop Panics from continuing to happen. The Stock Exchange crashed during the Panic of 1901, though the country recovered fairly quickly. During the Panic of 1907, President Teddy Roosevelt ordered that more greenbacks (which were not redeemable by either gold or silver) be printed to ease the money crunch. Banks still failed.

Finally, in 1933, during the throes of the Great Depression, President Franklin Roosevelt decreed that not only could ordinary citizens own gold bars and coins, but paper currency could not be used to redeem gold from the U.S. currency. (Silver was exempted, technically putting the country back on the Silver Standard.) Roosevelt's action sent the country closer to *fiat currency*, where paper money could be printed without concern whether it could all be redeemed by the U.S. or not. In 1971, President Nixon completed the action by exempting silver, as well. As of this writing, no country in the world bases their monetary system on either a gold or silver standard. Fiat currency reigns.

*William Jennings Bryan and wife*

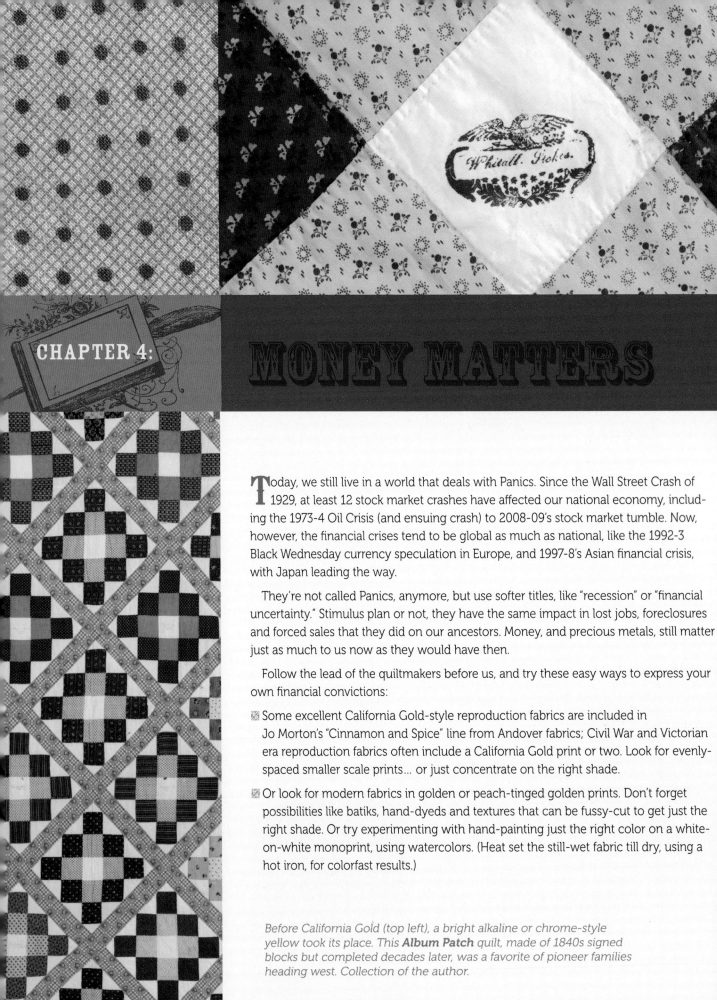

# CHAPTER 4: MONEY MATTERS

Today, we still live in a world that deals with Panics. Since the Wall Street Crash of 1929, at least 12 stock market crashes have affected our national economy, including the 1973-4 Oil Crisis (and ensuing crash) to 2008-09's stock market tumble. Now, however, the financial crises tend to be global as much as national, like the 1992-3 Black Wednesday currency speculation in Europe, and 1997-8's Asian financial crisis, with Japan leading the way.

They're not called Panics, anymore, but use softer titles, like "recession" or "financial uncertainty." Stimulus plan or not, they have the same impact in lost jobs, foreclosures and forced sales that they did on our ancestors. Money, and precious metals, still matter just as much to us now as they would have then.

Follow the lead of the quiltmakers before us, and try these easy ways to express your own financial convictions:

Some excellent California Gold-style reproduction fabrics are included in Jo Morton's "Cinnamon and Spice" line from Andover fabrics; Civil War and Victorian era reproduction fabrics often include a California Gold print or two. Look for evenly-spaced smaller scale prints... or just concentrate on the right shade.

Or look for modern fabrics in golden or peach-tinged golden prints. Don't forget possibilities like batiks, hand-dyeds and textures that can be fussy-cut to get just the right shade. Or try experimenting with hand-painting just the right color on a white-on-white monoprint, using watercolors. (Heat set the still-wet fabric till dry, using a hot iron, for colorfast results.)

*Before California Gold (top left), a bright alkaline or chrome-style yellow took its place. This **Album Patch** quilt, made of 1840s signed blocks but completed decades later, was a favorite of pioneer families heading west. Collection of the author.*

24

- Add a zing of California Gold to your scrap or planned scrap quilts. Used in small amounts, it adds contrast and glows against darker sashing and background combinations, like the darker brown pebble texture print in Golden Years (see page 106).

- Use California Gold in larger amounts to frame and define areas, particularly those surrounding darker patches. (See Turkey Tracks on page 116 for a good example.)

- Include gold or silver metallic prints in your regular mix of fabrics – for whichever Standard you lean toward (or mix in both to emphasize your equalitarian nature). Gold and silver often act as neutrals – gold for warmer-toned fabrics, silver for cooler tones.

- Look for money-themed prints, like the dollar bill print used for a sashing in Moneybags (see page 112). Game-themed fabric lines, like Monopoly, often use at least one money-type print. Other countries' currency prints are fair game as well, and show how cosmopolitan you are.

- Add coin-shaped buttons, charms or fringe to album or Crazy quilts. Embellishments can also include houses, cars and other symbols of our financial cares – airplanes, occupation symbols... even tiny cellphones and suitcases! Memory quilts of this time period will also benefit from financial touches, like a sheaf of paper "funny money," or a line of coin buttons pointing down to a dollar sign printed on fabric. If you can't find the right embellishment, make your own by hot-gluing dimes, nickels and pennies on pinbacks or shank buttons. (Foreign coins work, too.)

- Look for photos of your favorite political figures that can be used for photo-transfers. (Copyright issues may apply here unless you took the photo, so take care.) Many politicians and public figures have commemorative pins, handkerchiefs and t-shirts associated with them. (The "Hope" t-shirt featuring presidential candidate Barack Obama is a prime example.) These are perfect additions to memory quilts, Crazy quilts or traditional patchwork, either cut up, folded, tacked on or used as a quit back. Pins can be used as specialty accents, or displayed on a wallhanging while they're not being worn.

- Finally, give your own view on the Standard response by including one – just one – bright gold accent patch in your latest scrap quilt. (Add a note, written in permanent marker on muslin, stitched on the quilt back, explaining just what that patch symbolically represents.)

Express your opinion in your quilts and textile projects! Not only does it add a fun (and contemporary) touch to your work, but it gives you a chance to tell others what you think... about life, about our crazy, mixed-up, fascinating world. That sort of freedom is worth more than all the money – including gold and silver – in the world.

*Top right, a California Gold hexagon snuggles into a c.1890 Charm quilt top. Collection of the author.*

*Left, Double-sided Sixteen Patch/Crazy quilt, c.1889. The Crazy-patched side of this scrap quilt features a variety of California Gold scraps – but so does the Sixteen Patch side! A group of friends and family from Maine is thought to have made this piece; their names and dates are scattered throughout the Crazy top. Collection of Rocky Mountain Quilt Museum.*

*Bottom right, Paper money in denominations less than a dollar was not uncommon in early 19th century America – many banks printed their own bills.*

# A TIMELINE FOR THE GOLDEN WEST

**1785** U.S. sets up a silver standard, based on the Spanish milled dollar.

**1792** U.S. Mint established (Coinage act) –U.S. begins minting coinage.

**1828** America's first gold rush – in Lumpton County, GA (gold discovered in other states before this).

**1836** John Marsh arrives in California from Minnesota, becomes a doctor, and amasses a huge cattle herd. He writes many letters to newspapers further east, urging settlers to come to California. The Western Emigration Society is formed (*See Nancy Kelsey on page 60*).

**1837** May 10 Panic of 1837 – based in part on real estate speculation. Every bank stops payment in gold and silver coin. (Five years of depression follow).

**1839 May 1** Eighteen men from Peoria, IL set out for Oregon. (Nine actually make it.)

**July 1** John Sutter arrives in Yerba Buena (San Francisco), CA.

**1841** November 4 The Bartleson-Bidwell Company arrives at Dr. Marsh's ranch – the first overland party of emigrants to head west (half the party leaves at Soda Springs, ID and heads to the Williamette Valley in Oregon).

Early 1840s: Gold placer deposits begin to peter out in Georgia.

**1843** The Great Migration begins on the Oregon Trail.

**1846** Bear Flag Revolt – Californians try to form a republic.

**1847** January 13 Mexico gives up claims to California (Cahuenga Capitulation).

**1848** January 18-20 (sometime during this date) James W. Marshall discovers gold at Sutter's Fort.

**1848 California Gold Rush begins.**

Independent Treasury Act – U.S. coinage separated from banking system.

**1849** Biggest influx of emigrants to California's Gold Rush – and the Forty-Niners.

**1850** Spring Gold discovered in Gold Canyon, Nevada by Mormons on their way to the California Gold Rush.

**1857** Spring Comstock Silver Lode discovered near Virginia

**1857** Spring Comstock Silver Lode discovered near Virginia City, NV – but not publicized until it is taken over by Henry Comstock in 1858.

Summer Spanish-speaking gold seekers pan out gold in Denver area.

Sept. 11 SS Central America sinks.

Panic of 1857 Banks suspend payment in silver (caused in part by Central America's loss of millions of dollars in gold).

**1858** July Green Russell and Sam Bates discover a gold deposit in Englewood, CO.

**Pikes Peak Gold Rush begins.**

**1859** January 7 George Jackson discovers gold near Idaho Springs, CO. The highest point of the Pikes Peak Gold Rush – and the Fifty-Niners.

**1861** U.S. suspends payment in gold and silver (again).

**1861-2** Demand notes – first official U.S. paper money denominations ($5, $10 and $20 *greenbacks*).

**1861-5** U.S. Civil War.

**1863** Silver discovered in New Mexico.

**1864** Silver discovered in Montana (Phillipsburg).

**1869** May 10 Transcontinental Railroad completed (golden spike driven at Promontory, Utah) – after the Pacific Railroad Act of 1862, and seven years before the act's 1876 deadline.

**1873** **1876** **1877** **1878** **1882** **1890** **1891** **1882** **1893** **1896** **1898** **1907** **1914** **1918** **1929** **1933** **1939** **1941** **1959** **1971** **1973** **1980** **1987** **1989** **1990** **1992** **1997** **2003** **2007**

**1873** Coinage Act of 1873 enacted – de-monetizing silver and establishing the Gold Standard.

Panic of 1873 (four years of depression follow).

Silver veins found in Butte, MT.

Colorado's largest silver district discovered in Leadville.

**1876** U.S. Centennial.

**June 25-26** Custer's Last Stand (Battle of the Little Bighorn).

**1876** Lake Valley silver deposits found by a rancher in Sierra County, NM.

**1877** Copper discovered in Bisbee, AZ (near Tombstone), by a soldier chasing Apache Indians (silver is a valuable by-product).

**1878** Bland-Allison Act – requires US Treasury to purchase domestic silver bullion to be minted into legal coins.

**1882** Copper veins found in Butte... and copper quickly becomes the primary metal (silver remains a by-product).

**1890** Sherman Purchase Act –requires the government to buy millions of ounces of silver.

**1891** Gold discovered in Cripple Creek, CO –

**Final Colorado gold rush begins.**

W.S. Stratton discovers the Independence Lode near Victor, CO.

**1892** Grover Cleveland (pro-Gold standard) a Democrat, wins the presidential election.

**1893** Panic of 1893 – caused by bank and railroad failures, as well as the fight between goldbugs and silverites. Many silver millionaires ruined.

**1896** Free Silver, along with the Populist Party, aligns with the Democratic Party (William Jennings Bryan its presidential candidate).

**1898**: April – August - Spanish-American War.

**1901**: Panic of 1901 (Stock Exchange Crashes).

**1907**: Panic of 1907 – caused by bank failures.

**1914-18**: World War I.

**1918**: Anaconda Copper Mine produces open-pit copper until 1978 (near Yerington, NV).

**1929**: Oct. 24-28 Stock Market Crash.

Great Depression officially begins (though farmers have been dealing with crop failures and economic troubles through the 1920s).

**1933**: The U.S. goes off the gold standard – President Roosevelt announces that all citizens turn in their gold.

The U.S. announces that it will still issue paper money redeemable in silver coins and bullion – thus technically keeping the U.S. on the silver standard.

**1939-45**: World War II.

**1941**: U.S. officially enters WWII.

**1959-75**: Vietnam War.

**1971**: President Richard Nixon announces the U.S. will no longer redeem its paper notes for gold or any other precious metal – thus taking America off the gold standard (or any standard, for that matter).

**1973**: Oil crisis (leads to 1973-74 stock market crash).

**1980s**: Latin American debt crisis.

**1987**: Black Monday – largest one-day percentage drop in stock market history.

**1989-91**: U.S. Savings and Loan Crisis.

**1990-1**: Persian Gulf War.

**1990s**: Japanese assets and prices collapse.

**1992-3**: Black Wednesday – currency speculation in Europe.

**1997-8**: Asian Financial Crisis.

**2003**- Iraq War (Second Persian Gulf War).

**2007-9**: American Financial Crisis and Recession.

Credit cards began in the 1920s, offered so consumers wouldn't have to make a special trip to the bank to pay for gasoline or goods. In 1950, the Diners Club issued a cardboard card for use in 27 New York City restaurants; it had 20,000 customers within a year. In 1958, American Express created its first credit card; 60,000 BankAmericards (now known as Visas) were mailed out the same year to residents of Fresno, CA.

# GENERAL PATTERN INSTRUCTIONS

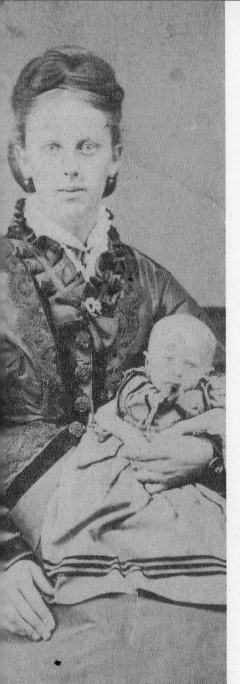

*Before You Begin: Read through the pattern!
Take a careful look at the options. Now you can make the quilt your way.

## *Quiltmaking 101:
We can all use a refresher course in basic quiltmaking techniques. Taking a class may help, either from a skilled local teacher or a national one. (Ask your friends, or a friendly clerk at the local quilt shop, who's helped them the most.) Internet sites are another place to check for helpful diagrams and advice. A number of books are excellent helps, as well – one personal favorite is Marianne Fons and Liz Porter's *Quiltmaker's Complete Guide*.

## *Choosing Fabrics, the Golden West Way

Many quilters prefer all-cotton fabrics for their soft touch and wearability. Old-time quilters primarily used cottons, although they also made charm quilts (and Crazies) from silk and "art silk" (artificial silk) fabrics. (Wool fabrics made occasional appearances in Log Cabins and Crazies, too.) They used scraps from family sewing, but were able to purchase scrap bags of leftover fabrics from manufacturers on occasion, too. Dry goods stores and eventually mail order businesses like Montgomery Ward also carried bolts of fabrics to choose from. Dyes were available not only to dye muslin, but re-dye faded fabrics. (Prints and solids were not always reliably colorfast in those days.)

Your easiest choice of fiber today is cotton, but don't hesitate to add scraps that may have a little polyester included. They won't hurt a thing. Follow the lead of your forbears, though, and mix in older fabrics – the more, the merrier! Antique scrap quilts used dozens – or hundreds – of different fabrics, ranging through the decades. You can, too, by purchasing fat eighths and fat quarters of fabric; mixed scrap bags; or trading with others.

Antique quilts often rely primarily on smaller-scale prints, like calicoes. California Gold prints – at least those examples found, so far – are all small-scale, usually polka dots, dashes, or other small geometric shapes on a golden background. It's not a bad idea to include large, medium and small-scale prints and weaves in your fabric choices, but let the small scale ones predominate.

*Dutch Triangles*, c.1885.
*The brighter golds in this scrap top
are "cheddars," a shade contemporary
with the softer California Golds.
Collection of Kathleen Litwinow.*

# Adding Your Own California Gold:

Authentic 1880s California Gold fabrics, aren't exactly waiting on the shelves, although they can be found here and there on eBay or several other venues, including antique malls, fairs and flea markets. However, you can approximate California Gold and other period fabrics with modern-made ones. Several reproduction fabric lines, like Jo Morton's "Cinnamon and Spice" series from Andover Fabrics, have California Gold look-alikes. Keep a lookout for soft gold or yellow small prints, especially those with 'caramel' shading. Peach-toned golds are also effective. For Gold Standard quilts, choose the brightest-contrast gold you can find, preferably a solid.

# What Colors Did They Use?

Since the California Gold prints predominate in the 1880s and early 1890s, quilts using California Gold often include the favorite shades of that period: greens, darker rose "madder" bubblegum pinks, soft blues and manganese "Hershey" browns (the same color as a Hershey's chocolate bar wrapper). These are often accompanied by "mourning" grays and blacks; indigo blues; "cheddar" yellows and golds, soft lavenders and dark purples, as well as scarlets and burgundys (the two were thought to offset each other, and were frequently mixed).

# Why So Much Muslin?

Creamy white solids predominate in this book's quilts. They're none other than muslin, that sturdy, reasonably-priced cotton that was the quilter's favorite in previous decades. Muslin was cheap and even free if cloth feed, sugar and flour sacks could be reused. Also, it acted as a visual equalizer when stitching with a wide range of scrap fabrics. Muslin could be dyed in various colors to make borders and sashing, and used as a background to stretch expensive prints further. When in doubt, use muslin.

However, you can add even more visual interest to your modern-made quilts by substituting white-on-white or white-on-cream prints, also called monoprints. From a distance, they look like muslin solids – but closer up, you'll notice the prints' tiny designs. (Girls of the Golden West's color version, for example, has little roses printed in a white-on-cream print, as a complementary touch to the Wild Rose quilting.)

Muslin can act as a neutral background for ironing photo-transfers, or tracing patterns for painting or embroidery. Considering how many uses it has, and how many fabrics it goes with, keeping a little muslin around is a wise thing.

## To Wash, Or Not to Wash

Should you wash quilt fabrics before using them? Quilters who value the 'new' feel and look will often cut and use their fabrics straight from the bolt. Quilters who are working with a wider mix of fabrics worry about things like dye bleeding and mixing different prints, so race home to wash everything first.

**Who's right? They both are.** The key is consistency. If you prefer unwashed fabrics, keep them that way – but test for colorfastness by brushing a damp q-tip across their surfaces. (If any color appears on the q-tip, that fabric is apt to bleed.) If you wash, use a mild soap solution or a baby detergent like Ivory. Line or iron dry, then store, separated by color.

# Making a Statement in Fabric

Metallics are a perfect complement to quilts with gold, silver and copper themes. If you can't find the right print, make it by embellishing your fabrics with a permanent metallic marker, or swirl of metallic fabric paint. (A light mist of spray fabric paint adds an overall shimmer without detracting.)

Also, look for prints with specialty designs, like the dollar bill print used as a sashing in the Moneybags quilt. Dollar signs, coin prints, prints that commemorate important events like elections, wars or emergencies (like 9/11), communicate your opinion without saying a word. If you can't find the right fabric, make your own, using an extra-fine point marker (fabric markers or Sharpie brand markers work well). Sketch small dollar signs, exclamation points or other insignias randomly across a piece of cream or colored solid. (A light-colored batik or texture print adds more interest.) You can also trace or photo-transfer the outline of a famous leader. (Use newspaper photos as a guide.) Don't hesitate to add bits and pieces of other textiles like handkerchiefs, dish towels, specialty ties, and such, if they follow the theme.

**Tip:** Boston-style "Tea Parties" are popular currently to protest taxes or government use of funds. Taking the lead of our Revolutionary War era ancestors, who dumped boxes of expensively-taxed tea in Boston Harbor, these protestors will often throw tea bags or sip tea to make their point. Add your opinion by including teapot or cup-themed prints in your fabrics. Or stitch on a teapot or teabag brass charm here and there, as a newsworthy embellishment.

*Courthouse Steps, c.1885. A Log Cabin variation, named for the many strips that formed its "stepping stone" look. Collection of the Rocky Mountain Quilt Museum.*

## *Ha-Ha Fabrics:* Enjoy a good joke? (Or driving an appraiser crazy?)

Include authentic old fabrics in your modern-made quilts! If you're using a 19th century quilt pattern, as many of these designs are, it's a secret pleasure to include at least a few 19th century fabrics as part of the mix. The color version of Girls of the Golden West, for example, uses real 1880s California Gold fabric yardage, found on eBay, for the alternating blocks and triangles, as well as the accent squares. You don't have to use quite so much – a patch or two will have the same effect. Cut them from a damaged quilt top or orphan block, if you don't have 19th century yardage laying around in your stash. (!!!) Fabric scraps are available from places like eBay, antique and thrift shops. (Eileen Trestain's books on fabric identification are an excellent resource; you may also find this author's Fabric Dating Kit helpful.) Stitch the fabrics in place. Ask friends, "Ok, where are the old fabrics?" Then gloat!

## *Figuring Yardage*

This requires a little math, some finagling...and patience. But it's worth it, to get the maximum amount of use out of your fabric. As a magazine editor, this quilter did a lot of patterning and figuring yardages. A few steps help you through it:

1. **Isolate your basic block(s).** Now figure how many patches – of what type – are in each block. List the patches on a paper, one by one, including how much space each patch fits into. (The A and B leaves on Turkey Tracks, for example, fit in a 1 1/2" x 4 1/2" space, approximately, including seam allowances.) Multiply the patch figures by the total number of blocks in the quilt.

2. **What fabrics do you plan to use?** Turkey Tracks, for example, uses a green print, a red print, California Gold – and muslin. If you plan to use a variety of fabrics, list them by shade (light, medium, dark) or by dominant colors, as "Scraps."

3. **Figure the width of a fabric as 40".** (Fabrics are often 42"-44" wide, so any extra is 'gravy.') Figure the patches needed as follows, starting with the largest first.

Let's say you need four 4" x 73" border strips, plus 80 - 2" patches, all from green print.

## Here's how to do it:

Sketch a width of fabric on your paper, then draw a horizontal line under it. Write '4"' on the width – but you need 2 widths (i.e., 8" total) for each border strip (at least 7" x 4" will be leftover from width #2). So for 4 border strips, you need 8 widths: 8 x 4" = 32." (Note: If you want a full border strip without piecing it, you'll have to plan to buy at least 73" – 2 1/8 yards – so you can cut the border strips vertically. That leaves plenty of yardage to cut other patches.)

The 2" patches are next – all 80 of them. Sketch another chunk across the fabric width, block off a series of squares, and write '2" in them. You can get 20 - 2" blocks across the width of the fabric – and since 80 total are needed, you need to cut 4 widths of 2". In other words, 4 x 2" = 8".

Almost done. You need 32" plus 8", for a total of 40". (Multiply this figure by 1.05%, for safety's sake.) Fabric is sold in the following increments:

| | |
|---|---|
| 1/8 yard = 4.5" | |
| 1/4 yard = 9.0" | |
| 1/3 yard = 12.0" | |
| 1/2 yard = 18.0" | |
| 5/8 yard = 22.5" | |
| 3/4 yard = 27" | |
| 7/8 yard = 31.5" | |
| 1 yard = 36" | |

Round up your numbers to the nearest increment. In other words, for 40", you need 1 1/4 yards of fabric. Add an extra 1/4 or 1/2 yard, if you're nervous, uncertain or working with a large amount of patches that need to be cut from just one fabric.

You need to do these measurements for every patch in your quilt, plus backing and binding – but once it's done, you have a solid idea of how much yardage is needed to make the quilt. (See *Batting and Backing* on pages 36-38 for more on figuring for those items.)

## *Cutting Tools

Our pioneer foremothers would have killed for the convenience of a rotary cutter and mat! As it was, they generally cut their patches out using a template of some kind – made from tin, wood or heavy paper – traced on the fabric, then cut out with scissors. (They were not unfamiliar with strip piecing, but generally used that technique more when making Log Cabin or string-pieced quilts.) You can also make your quilt this way, of course, but it takes longer and has a higher tendency to be inaccurate than rotary cutting. (On the other hand, you can cut a whole line of rotary patches wrong in one swoop!) Whatever your tool, keep it sharp for best results.

**Tip:** If you're making multiples of the same pieced unit, take the cue of our foremothers, and make a template (cut size, not finished size). Use it to double-check your pieced units; if they're off-sized, trim to fit, taking a bit off each side as needed.

**Tip:** Cutting tables are hard on taller quilters' backs. Not literally, of course, but the constant bending over can really make you stiff and sore! Save the cost of a trip to the back doctor by investing in specialized blocks that raise your cutting table to a comfortable height. Similar blocks can also be found just before college semesters begin; they're often used to raise dorm beds so storage space can be created underneath. (Another idea for that blank storage left underneath *your* table!) Bricks, pavers and even cut chunks of board can substitute. (This quilter's dad built a convenient wooden 'lip' around her board extenders, so the table legs wouldn't accidentally slip off.) A godsend for basting quilts, too.

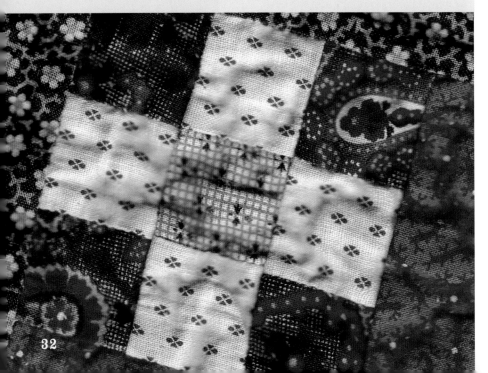

*Framed Nine Patch* detail, see page 100.

## *Handwork versus Machine Work

Nearly all the blocks in 19th century quilts are hand-stitched...but not all the block joins. Good hand sewing skills were considered the trademark of a clever, accomplished lady. The sewing machine, however, was beginning to be manu-factured in larger quantities by the early 1850s, though, and quilters were fascinated by this newfangled machine. Some machine-stitched and/or quilted pieces were made, but most women could not afford a machine of their own for decades. In the meantime, they continued to hand sew.

It seems safe to say that more 19th century quilts would have been machine stitched *if* sewing machines were more available and affordable. Machines were borrowed or rented throughout communities occasionally, and it is not that un-common to find quilts whose blocks are joined by machine – or the bindings topstitched in place by machine. The c.1855-60 Civil War Era Sampler on page 125 even includes machine quilting! See "Sewing Machine History" on page 51 for more.

*Golden History Quilt, 1992. Volunteers from the museum designed this piece to commemorate Golden, Colorado's rich mining history. From the collection of the Rocky Mountain Quilt Museum.*

# *Piecing Your Quilt

Even, straight stitches, whether you do them by hand or machine, are very, very impor-tant. For machine piecing, make sure you have an accurate ¼" seam allowance. (Some stitchers prefer the width of the presser foot.) What is important: you need to use the same seam allowance throughout the quilt.

Hand stitching can be easier for small unit piecing. It can also be very accurate, especially if you mark stitching lines on each patch. Some hand-piecers, like Jinny Beyer, think that 1/4" is too wide for a seam allowance; they prefer 1/8". Hand piecing is portable, too...but it takes a while to accomplish.

Don't hesitate to mix hand and machine piecing on these patterns, if that accomplishes your project faster or more accurately. It's been done many a time.

## *Piecing Triangle Squares:

There are many different ways to cut and sew triangles. This book shows you two of the traditional methods – how to cut a square diagonally to get two triangles, or diagonally both ways to get four triangles. We've also provided a graph method – a whole page of marked squares that can be stitched, then cut, using the paper-marked lines as a guide. (See page 53 for help.) Other methods may work bet-ter for you, or give faster results. (For example, mark a diagonal line on a top square, then match it with a bottom square. Stitch 1/4" on either side of the diagonal line, then cut right on the marked line. Press. Voila, you have two triangle-pieced squares!) It's not the method that matters for this; it's the size. Use "Triangle Rules" on page 45 for help with figuring.

# *Appliquéing Your Quilt

Today's appliqué tends to be 'invisible.' Stitches are tucked under the fabric, using fine or silk thread to minimize showing. Old-time appliquérs would not have understood this – after all, how can you prove your stitching is strong, if it doesn't show? (They left knots visible on the top of the quilt, for the same reason.)

Motifs were often anchored with cream-colored whipstitching, one after the other, that left a ridged edge around each patch. By the end of the 19th century, appliqué stitching was more inobtrusive, but stitches showed more then than they do today.

Patch edges are traditionally turned under and basted in place before appliquéing can begin. Although old-time quilters were unfamiliar with it, fusibles can also be used to do your appliqué work.

A general quiltmaking book (See **Quiltmaking 101**, page 28) can walk you through appliqué methods, or try books by Ami Simms or Elly Sienkiewicz.

Decorative appliqué, much of it anchored with buttonhole stitch embroidery, became especially popular in the early 20th century. Buttonhole appliqué is still popular today, and used to anchor traditional and fused appliqué alike.

## *The Importance of Ironing:
Many a famous quilter's reputation has been made in part from careful ironing! It is difficult to downplay the importance of this step, especially with smaller-sized pieces, like the triangle squares in State of the Union or Girls of the Golden West. Want to be admired for your work, too? These tips may help.

## *Fabric starch is important.
It helps smooth pieced and appliquéd seams, and gives lighter fabrics more body. Recent articles have suggested that starch draws bugs toward quilts. This quilter has never had that problem – but if you're worried (especially if you live in the southern states), rinse your finished quilt top or quilt to remove the starch.

*Keep a spray water bottle handy to banish wrinkles or smooth out fabrics. A few drops of lavender or lemon scent add a nice touch.

*Start from the back.

*Use the point of the iron along the seamline as you push the seams gently in one direction, generally (but not always) toward the darker fabrics. If the seam is caught, clip it slightly, then push in the direction of the others.

*The back of your work should look as tidy as the front. Want good results? This is critical.

*Now go to the front of your piece. Make sure everything is flat, and seams are fully extended. (No folds or puckers, if possible.) Let the piece cool slightly before using. If you're working with a photo-transferred area, don't iron directly on that surface – it may stick. (Turn it over, and iron on the back, instead.)

*As you stitch, finger press (push or scratch the seams down with your fingernail) every seam – or iron every other seam. Getting up to use the iron is a pain, but it is exercise! (You can also keep a small iron near your sewing machine.)

**Take longer to iron, and do it carefully– you won't regret it.**

**I can't get my seams to match!** The 'ridge' method works best for this quilter, and it may help you, too. As you're matching sewn patches, feel carefully – when the seams are lined up with each other, you feel a 'ridge' under your fingertips. Put a pin just to the left or right of that ridge to help keep the seamlines pushed together. (Not right on the seam – that encourages distortion.) Once the seam is sewn, press it back before continuing. Good ironing skills can salvage many a "boo-boo."

**My pieced triangle points are blunted!** For nice crisp points, start with the back of your pieced triangle square strips. Press the block joins so they face away from each print triangle – that way, your joined stitchlines make a large X. Sew through the middle of each X, taking care to keep your stitched line as even as possible. Press the strips on both front and back, gently pushing back any extra-fold or rolled-over seams.

**My pieced border strips are too long/short!** The trouble is probably in one of two areas: either your patches were miscut (at least some of them), or your seam allowances are slightly off. The best way to deal with this is proactive: *measure your pieced triangle squares **before** sewing with them.* Trim any squares that are off-sized, taking care to trim a little off each side, if at all possible. Set aside any too-small pieced squares for another project.

*Above, another look at the Crazy side of the Double-Sided Sixteen Patch/Crazy Quilt (see page 25.)*

**What – you don't want to take those strips apart?** (The seam ripper is not the quilter's most loved – and hated – tool for no reason!)

**If the strips are too long,** shorten them by re-sewing the block joins, but taking a slightly deeper seam allowance on each as you go. Re-press, then match and pin back in place.

**If the strips are too short,** re-sew the joins, but with a slightly smaller seam allowance. (Pick out the old stitching threads, and re-press.) Spray starch and pulling gently as you press are often enough to stretch a little extra length out, too.

**My strip-pieced Nine Patch blocks are unraveling!** Pieced strip sets need to have strong seams – so increase your stitch-per-inch measurement to 10-13. Be sure to use good-quality thread, too.

**My borders don't fit – or they're rippling!** It's possible that your seam allowances were slightly off throughout the quilt, leading to a smaller or larger top than the pattern suggested. It's also possible that your borders were not cut correctly. In either case, re-measure your top through the center, both vertically and horizontally, and use those measurements to trim your border strips to size. If your border is rippling, you most likely stretched or pulled on it while fitting and stitching it in place.

One way to deal with this is to remove the border and re-stitch it, gently smoothing as you go, rather than pulling. Another is an old quilt restorer's trick: hand-baste around the border's edge, then gently pull on the thread until the border fabric lays flat. Quilt or tie, then sew on the first binding seam just **inside** the line of basting threads. Trim, then finish binding your quilt.

## *Batting and Backing for Your Quilt: What did older quilters use for their batting and quilt backings?

Hands-on, it was almost always cotton batting and cotton muslin backings. Many a scrap quilt from the California Gold period used sugar or flour sacks, laid flat and stitched together. If you like that effect, use plain feedsacks picked up from eBay, an antique mall or garage sale; you generally need four large ones, stitched together. (Another possibility: good-condition old kitchen dishtowels, which were also often made from old feedsacks.) Or find the best-quality modern muslin and use that.

## Batting Notes:

Some Western states, like Idaho, had more access to sheep than cotton fields. Out of necessity, they used what they had. In that case, you'll want to look for wool batting, instead of cotton. In any case, a bonded batting helps keep the fibers from separating as the quilt gets older. An increasing number of quilters also prefer an "80/20" mixed batting of cotton and polyester; this batt has the soft look and flat feel of cotton, but is easier to stitch on and stays together longer. It's your choice.

**How much should I get?** You need a batting/backing that is at least 4" larger all the way around, to cope with shrinkage and shifting. It's not difficult to figure.

For example, let's assume you're working with a 66" x 72" top. That means you need a 70" x 76" batting/backing piece. For the batting, cut the piece needed, or 'wed' two pieces by hand-thinning the edges where they join. (Gently pull until the batting thins, then slightly overlap one piece on the other. Baste in place, if needed; usually the two will stick to each other.)

If you have extra-wide 'quilt backing' fabric on hand, you're a lucky person – just cut the backing size needed. Often, though, you'll have to piece 2 or 3 widths of fabric together. Do the math, adding at least 1/2" for each piece of fabric, for seam allowances. In the case of our example quilt, if your fabric is 42" or less wide (most are), you need 2 widths of fabric at least 66" long. Cut 2 - 36 1/2" x 66" panels and stitch together.

## *Basting Your Quilt:

To help you visualize the whole process, think of this step as making a quilt "sandwich," with the backing and pieced top enclosing a meaty "filling" of batting. (!!!) Find a large smooth area – some people use a long table, others prefer a clean stretch of carpet or hardwood floors. Push family pets outside so they don't feel the need to "help."

Lay out the backing fabric, stretching it gently so it's as smooth as possible. Lay batting on top, smoothing as you go. Center and add the pieced top. Keep all three layers as smooth as you can.

**Tip:** Some quilters literally tape the backing fabric to whatever they're laying it on – they feel it gives them smoother final results. Scotch tape or double-stick carpet tape work, and aren't as difficult to pry up as that sturdy "handyman's secret weapon," duct tape. However, all three tapes may leave a residue on both stretching area and stretched fabric, so make sure they're taped sparingly on an edge that will be trimmed away.

*Detail, c.1890 **Triangle Charm** quilt, collection of the author.*

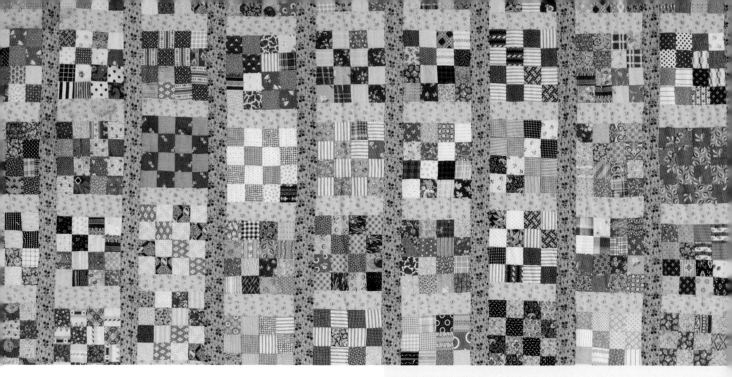

*The **Sixteen Patch** side of the **Double-Sided Sixteen Patch/Crazy Quilt**, (see page 25.)*

Time to begin basting! Many quilters use large safety pins to "pin-baste" their quilts, approximately 3-4" apart in all directions. After trying pin-basting for years with indifferent (or even worse, bad) results, this quilter has found herself going back to the old way – thread basting. For her, at least, thread-basted quilts stay smoother, with fewer ripples, folds and catches in the finished product. Try it once for yourself, and see what works for you.

For thread basting, you need a large-eyed quilting or sewing needle, plus a spool of cheap thread, patience and a clean pair of jeans. Thread the needle with a long hank of thread, then beginning in the middle, start basting, taking long stitches (4-5") through all three layers in a sort of running stitch all the way to the outside of the quilt. *(Yes, this means you may have to crawl across the surface of the quilt occasionally, if you're on the floor. Keep the quilt layers as smooth and even as possible.)* Continue stitching in parallel lines, approximately 3-4" apart, all across the surface of the quilt. When you run out of thread, tie a fresh hank of thread onto your basted threadline, thread the needle, and resume stitching. Keep on until the quilt is completely basted.

In either case, remove the pins or threads as you quilt…or after the quilt is finished, but before binding.

**Tip:** Do you belong to a church, civic group…or a quilting guild? Know of a nearby quilt shop? In many cases, you can borrow their long banquet or teaching tables to baste your quilt. Put two tables together, then spread the quilt "sandwich" out, as described above. Walk around the table edges as needed to baste across the quilt surface. Ask your friends to help – or baste more than one quilt at the same time. For some years, this quilter taught an ongoing class to a group at a retirement community. The women in that group, dubbed the "Wild Things," set aside a time every month specifically for basting members' projects. Two members threaded needles; the others positioned themselves at the quilt sides or corners, and stitched as quickly as they could, grabbing fresh-threaded needles as they went. A queen-sized quilt sometimes took as little as an hour to baste, done this way!

# *Quilting Your Quilt

Hand quilting was by far the most common choice for quilting, though old-time quilters would also use machine quilting, especially for "useful" quilts. Generally, these styles of quilts were done in an overall pattern, like parallel lines, diamonds or checkerboards. You may prefer to outline-quilt motifs instead, and trace a pattern in the plain areas, like **Wild Rose** on page 44. General quiltmaking books can walk you through the process; state quilt and historical books, or quilting books (those by Helen Squire are excellent) are good sources of quilting motifs.

**Hand or machine quilting.** Which method is better? Historically, both happened during the Gold Rush period and beyond in the 19th century. It was far more common for quilts to be hand quilted, partly because handwork was important as a show of womanhood, and partly because sewing machines were still expensive – and scarce. (See Sewing Machine History on page 51 for more.) Technically speaking, sewing machine quilting stitches put far more holes in the fabric than hand quilting stitches. If you've included large amounts of vintage or antique fabric in your quilt, like the color version of Girls of the Golden West on page 40 (which uses authentic 1880s California Gold for setting squares and triangles), those fabrics will be under less stress with fewer stitch holes.

Honestly though, when working with modern materials, it doesn't matter. What is important – that the method is done well. Keep your stitches small and even, regardless of whether you hand quilt, or do it by machine.

## *Binding Your Quilt:
You want your binding to last…right? A double-fold French binding may take slightly more fabric, but it's easier to stitch accurately, thanks to the finished-line folded edge. And two layers of fabric protect better than one.

All the patterns in this book assume an approximately 1/4" French binding, cut on the straight grain. To make it, cut 2 1/4" strips the width of the fabric; you need enough to cover all of the quilt edges, plus 10" extra for turning corners. (For example, an 80" x 93" quilt would need 80 +

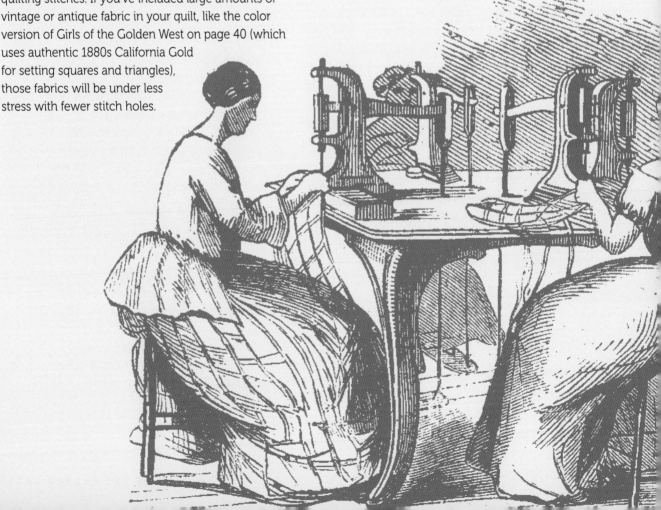

80 + 93 + 93 + 10 = 356".) Join the fabric strips, then fold and press lengthwise. Stitch the outer raw folded double edge in place first, mitering or rounding corners as you go. Trim any extra batting/backing away, leaving at least 1/2". Turn the folded finished edge over, stuffing it firmly as you go with the extra batting/backing. (This is one step many people skimp on, to their later regret.) Hand or machine stitch in place. A good general quiltmaking book can take you through the binding and corner mitering process, step by step.

**Tip:** Fine art is only complemented by a lovely frame, and your binding should have the same effect on your finished quilt. Choose a darker shade to visually "stop" the eye; texture prints or batiks are particularly effective. Plaids and stripes add texture and visual interest, but binding strips using these fabrics should be cut diagonally – in other words, on the bias. (One sad quilt in this quilter's collection has a "crooked" straight-grain plaid binding. It doesn't, but that doesn't matter – it *looks* as if it does.)

## Washing Your Quilt

There is a certain cachet about keeping your quilt in "unwashed condition" after you finish. This quilter, however, advocates giving it at least a quick rinse after the final stitch is taken. Why? Because the quilt has gathered surface soil and skin oil as you've worked on it. In the very long run, those items won't do the fabric any good. Also, rinsing the quilt will eliminate any blue marking lines for quilting, and will minimize other marking lines.

Try a mild solution of soap or baby detergent, with a few tablespoonfuls of borax thrown in. Unless you have a front-load machine, don't let it agitate your new quilt. Instead, turn the washing machine off and knead the quilt with your own hands. Turn to spin cycle, then let the machine go into rinse cycle, as well. Once the tub has filled, turn the machine off again, then knead and agitate with your own hands. Run through spin and rinse cycle a second time, and agitate with your hands. Then let it run through the final spin cycle to finish. See *"Ask Cindy"* on the Brickworks website, *www.cindybrick.com*, for soap amounts, plus a step-by-step explanation of the washing process.

**OLD QUILT BINDINGS ARE NOT WHAT YOU THINK.** Quilts from before the 1850s are fairly well bound – so are "best" quilts. But the average scrap quilt from the 19th century has a single-layer binding that looks as if it were stuffed on as an afterthought. Seams are barely turned under, loose edges peek out, and corners are finished in a variety of ways – including jamming in extra batting, then heavily whipstitching the edge. The results would make today's quilt judges faint with horror.

Why? Frankly, it's uncertain, but the reason may be practical. On any quilt, the binding takes the most use – and often wears out before the rest of the quilt. Why put a lot of extra care into a binding that would need to be replaced in a few years, anyways?

**GIRLS OF THE GOLDEN WEST**, *stitched by Bonnie DeVries and Cindy Brick, with help from Corrinn Cumings and Anne Heath. This new design was inspired by the antique State of the Union quilt shown on page 86.*

# GIRLS OF THE GOLDEN WEST

**Meet the Ladies** – feisty, independent women of West whose lives were changed by gold, silver and copper. They may gained it by being first on the spot – like Nancy Kelsey, whose wagon train was the first organized group to travel westward to California. (Nancy herself made a good bit of the trip trudging barefoot, her baby in her arms.) Sometimes they married men who struck it rich – like Elizabeth "Baby Doe" Tabor and Margaret "Molly" Brown. Sometimes they mined it themselves – like Ellen "Nellie" Cashman did in California, the Baja, Arizona and even the Klondike... or Fermina Sarras in Nevada...or Marie Pantalon in California. Or they just took it for themselves –like Belle Starr, one of the West's famous bandit queens.

Whatever their stories, these women have earned their places in the annals of the Golden West – and now on your quilt. See pages 56-77 for their amazing stories.

*Colorado mining girl, part of a series of state 'pinup' postcards, c.1905.*

# HOW TO MAKE GIRLS OF THE GOLDEN WEST

**FINISHED QUILT SIZE: 52" X 52" SQUARE (3 ROWS OF 3 - 13" BLOCKS, ON POINT)**

## FABRIC REQUIREMENTS

Assorted medium and dark fabric scraps (pieced triangle squares): 2 yards

California Gold 1 (accent squares in outer block pieced border): 1/4 yard

California Gold 2 (alternating squares, large setting triangles and corner triangles): 1 1/2 yard

Background fabric (muslin used in original quilt): 2 1/3 yards

Backing: 4 yards (cut 2 panels 28" x 59" and join vertically)

Batting: 59" x 59" square

Binding: 2/3 yard

## CUTTING REQUIREMENTS

### Blocks

**Pieced Blocks** (9 - 13" pieced blocks needed)

*Block Centers:* Photo-transfer (or trace and paint) the nine ladies on the cream fabric, leaving at least 2" extra all around. Center and cut each out as a 6 1/2" square.

**Tip:** Don't forget the 9-block composite (see page 46)! It will be a reminder of each person's name – and an excellent label for the quilt back.

*Pieced inner and outer 1" block borders:* Cut 2" squares from assorted med/dark scraps, then cut these in half diagonally; you'll need 36 squares per block, or a total of 324

squares. (Cut these into 648 triangles needed for the quilt.) Tip: Or use the quick-pieced triangle grid on page 53, plus instructions, for an even faster way to make these. Use as many different fabrics as possible, to preserve the scrappy look.

*California Gold 1" border accent squares:* From California Gold #1, cut 4 1 1/2" squares for each block, for a total of 36 squares.

*Inner block setting triangles:* From cream solid, cut a 8 1/4" square diagonally both ways to yield 4 triangles. (See Triangle Rule #2 on page 45 for help.) You'll need 9 - 8 1/4" squares, for a total of 36 triangles.

# How To Make A Photo-Transfer

Transferring a photo onto fabric isn't difficult if you follow a few basic steps.

First, choose a good-quality photo-transfer product – either one purchased for use in your computer printer, or one from a reputable sales outlet, like Kinko's. (I've worked with a printer in town for years, who supplies specialty paper I for use with their color photocopy machines.) If you'd prefer doing it on your own computer printer, I've been very pleased with the photo-transfer kits sold by Ami Simms *(http://www.amisimms.com)*, as well as Printed Treasures, printable cloth sheets sold at many quilt shops, as well as *http://www.softexpressions.com.*

Next, copy each 'lady' onto a photo-transfer sheet –but specify 'mirror image.' Trim the 'ladies' out, either as a square, or by following their outlines. Trim closely, but don't worry about extra space between the arm and body, or other close spaces. (Don't leave out Lotta's cigar or Marie's grapes!)

Now you're ready to transfer. If you're using a packaged kit, follow directions given – or ask the company what to do next. **Here's what I do:** choose a piece of cotton or polyblend abric that's at least 2" larger all around than the transfer motif. Iron that fabric so it's hot, then immediately put the transfer on, **face-down**, so it starts to bond. Now start ironing directly on the transfer, taking care to press firmly on every part, including the edges and corners. The paper I use takes between 40-70 seconds (I count), but your time may be longer or shorter, depending on which paper you're using. Gently start peeling away the paper; if you're seeing splotches and dots on the paper, it's not ready. Put the paper back down and iron 15-20 seconds longer. When you check again, the paper should peel away evenly. If the transfer's gotten wrinkled, it probably could have been ironed longer – but you can even out the wrinkles by ironing it **face-down** until smooth. Let the transferred cloth cool before you trim it to size.

**Alternating Blocks, Large Setting Triangles and Corner Triangles**
(4 - 13" finished blocks, 8 large setting triangles and 4 corner triangles needed)

From **California Gold** 2 fabric, cut 2 - 19 1/2" squares, then cut these diagonally both ways for 8 large setting triangles. (See the Triangle Rule #2 box on page 45 for help.) Then, cut 4 - 13 1/2" squares. Finally, cut 2 - 9 1/2" squares diagonally for 4 corner triangles.

Tip: **Floating Is Good!** People whose every stitch is accurate, no matter what – please disregard. For the rest of us, though, "floating" can be a very good thing. What it means: cut those large setting triangles and corner triangles slightly larger than what's absolutely needed – say, a 21" square cut diagonally both ways, instead of the size listed. This extra will produce a slightly larger space around the outside of the quilt, letting the blocks "float" a bit, rather than have them absolutely pinched into place. In the case of this quilt, it gives you the freedom to trim and bind your quilt top without worrying about cut-off block corner points.

# Backing, Batting and Binding

See General Instructions on pages 36-38.

# Block Assembly

### PIECED BLOCKS (13" FINISHED):

1. Stitch 2 scrap triangles together for a border triangle square; repeat until you have 44 squares for the outer border, and 28 for the inner border –a total of 72. Measure; these should be 1 1/2". Trim if needed. (The quick-pieced triangle square method on page 45 can also be used.)

   **Inner border:** sew 2 strips of 6 triangle squares, plus 2 strips of 8.

   **Outer border:** sew 4 strips of 5 triangle squares, and 4 of 6 squares. Set aside for later.

2. *Use the block diagram for help as you begin building the block.* **Inner border first:** join one 6-triangle square strips to either side of a 'lady' square, taking care to stitch as evenly as possible through the points. (Look for the X the back seams form, and stitch through the X centers.) Press. Now fit and stitch the 8-triangle square pieced strips to the remaining 2 sides. Press again.

3. **Setting Triangles:** starting on opposite sides, fit and stitch a setting triangle. Add and stitch on the remaining 2 triangles, then press.

**Tip:** *Check your measurements after you iron. Is the block approximately 13 1/2" square? If possible, trim the block slightly to fit – or plan to "fudge" by taking narrower seams or stretching the pieced units as you go.*

4. **Outer border:** pick up the reserved outer border pieced strips. Sandwich a **California Gold** square in between two of the 6 triangle-pieced square strips; stitch, then repeat for two border strips. Sandwich a California Gold square in between 2 – 5" triangle-square strips; repeat for the 2 shorter border strips.

5. Fit the shorter borders to the top and bottom of the block, using the central **California Gold** square as a guide. Stitch, then press. Repeat with the longer strips on the other 2 sides. This was your first block – and now it's done! Enjoy.

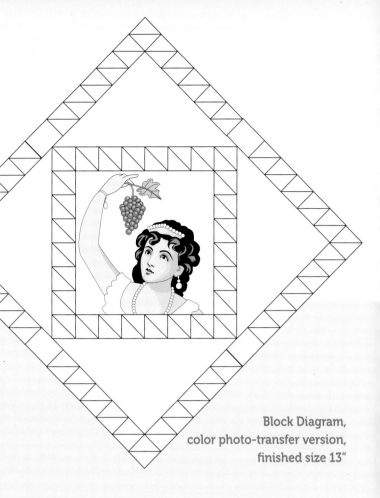

Block Diagram, color photo-transfer version, finished size 13"

**Tip:** *Leave a block out, so you can look at it while you sew the remaining blocks. It's much easier, and you'll be surprised at your speed while piecing the final block.*

6. Repeat for 8 more pieced blocks – a total of 9.

# Quilt Assembly

### STITCHING THE TOP

1. Lay out blocks in a 3 x 3 set on point, moving the 'ladies' around until you're happy with the overall balance. (Or arrange them as shown in the quilt photo, diagram and composite – it's up to you.)

2. Fit in the **California Gold** setting blocks, large triangles and corner triangles. (Use the quilt diagram for help.) Stitch, row by row, pressing as you go. Press the final quilt.

3. If your top is "floating," (see page 42) trim it evenly just before going on to the next step.

# Quilt Assembly CONT.

### FINISHING THE TOP

**Note:** The quilt diagram shown features an antique Wild Rose quilting motif that gives your quilt's straight lines and triangles a softer accent. If you'd like to use it, too, now's the time to trace both the full and partial motifs on the quilt top. Old-time quilters would have used chalk, or a pencil; a modern favorite is a blue washable quilt marker. Use what you like best – but if it's a pencil, try a very sharp mechanical pencil for good results. Layer your top with batting and backing; baste. Using cream thread, quilt the rose motifs, then outline the various pieced sections, as well as each Lady. Bind to finish the quilt.

**WILD ROSE QUILTING MOTIF:** *This is 6" tall, about 2/3 the size needed for the plain alternating blocks in Golden West Girls. Enlarge (using a photocopy machine) until you're pleased with the size, then trace it onto your plain blocks. For the fill-in triangles, use the same sized motif but only include the central roses and a leaf or two, like the example shown.*

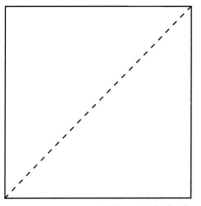

Triangle Rule 1:
Finished size + 7/8" (or 1") = cut size

Straight grain

Bias grain

Straight grain

Triangle Rule 1:
Bias grain on inside of triangles

# Triangle Rules

I learned about **Triangle Rules** when I was an editor at *Quilter's Newsletter*, and they have helped me ever since when figuring and cutting triangles.

Take a minute to photocopy this and post it near your cutting board – you won't regret it.

To cut 2 triangles from a square: actual finished size + 7/8" = cut square size.

Cut diagonally one way through the square, as shown.

(Even better — add 1" instead of 7/8", then trim pieced units slightly if needed – they'll be much more accurate overall)

Triangles cut this way will be bias on their cut (longest) edge. And bias tends to stretch, especially in larger triangles (like those on the outside of a quilt). To solve that issue...

To cut 4 triangles from a square: actual finished size x 1.5 = cut square size.

Cut diagonally both ways through the square, as shown.

Using this way, your bias edges will be on a shorter side – and the more stable straight grain edge will be on the cut (longest) side.

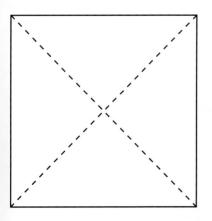

Triangle Rule 2:
Finished size x 1.5 = cut size

Bias grain

Straight grain

Straight grain

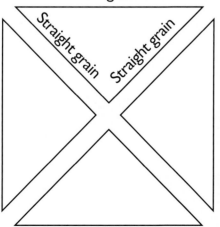

Triangle Rule 2:
Bias grain on outside of triangles

# Embellishment Options

Want to make the Ladies even more distinctive? Try adding beads, buttons, ribbon roses and other embellishments to their outfits! Use the details on their color illustrations as a starting point. Several have drawn laces or ruffles that can be over-stitched with the real thing. Or take Marie Pantalon's cue and add pearl trim on top of her necklace and tiara! (Marie's grapes would be yummy as little purple beads, grouped together.) Every one of the ladies, from Baby Doe's or Molly's hats (perfect for ribbon roses and/or feathers) to Lotta Crabtree's cigar (use a fat double row of brown chenille) would benefit from embellishments.

Let yourself expand into the rest of the quilt, too. Each and every corner could benefit from the addition of a charm or button – or scatter them randomly throughout the pieced triangle units. (Another thought: center them, one by one, in the California Gold squares in the blocks' outer borders.) These ladies weren't afraid to let go and try new possibilities – you should be, too.

BABY DOE TABOR

MOLLY BROWN

NANCY KELSEY

BELLE STARR

MARIE PANTALON

FERMINA SARRAS

LOTTA CRABTREE

EMILY WEST (NEE MORGAN)

NELLIE CASHMAN

**GIRLS OF THE GOLDEN WEST
BLOCK COMPOSITE.**

*Think of this also as a handy label to keep the ladies identified on the front when stitched c
quilt's back! It can be photo-transferred, or traced. In a pinch, make a photocopy of this pa
tuck it into a stitched pocket on the quilt back.*

Assembly Diagram

# GIRLS OF THE GOLDEN WEST REDWORK

**The Ladies can also be embroidered in all their glory, thanks to this redwork version of Girls of the Golden West.** Traditionally, this style is made in one color plus muslin, with the primary shade initially a vivid scarlet or Turkey red. Later on in the 19th century, brown/white and double pink/white quilts were not uncommon. This version picks another favorite combination: cobalt blue and white, and gives the pieced blocks a lacy effect against the background. It also adds a new element, taken from the original inspiration, the antique State of the Union quilt (see page 86): a 2" pieced triangle border all the way around the edge of the quilt.

Note: In this design, you'll be embroidering the Ladies, rather than photo-transferring them. Doing this isn't difficult at all. Start by tracing each Lady onto white fabric, using a sharp pencil or washable blue marker. (Use the finest point possible for best results.) Some like to make a photocopy, tape it on a window or lightbox, then position the fabric over top. (Be sure to add 2" extra all around – you'll trim to a square after embroidering.)

Use the Stitch Glossary (see pages 50-51) as a help to embroider each Lady, using two strands of embroidery floss for general work, and one strand (the Victorian stitcher's secret weapon) for delicate details, like faces and names. When you're done, dampen each and press carefully around the embroidery – then center and trim each to a 6 1/2" square.

## The History of Redwork

Although its heyday was in the later 19th and earlier centuries, redwork – technically outline stitch embroidery – started more as edging and decorative motifs on blouses and kitchen linens decades before. Dyes were notoriously unstable; since clothing and linens (quilts, too!) were often boiled to clean them, it was almost impossible to add anything pretty.

That all changed when the Turks introduced a bright, vivid red dye in the first part of the 19th century. By the 1830s, Turkey Red was in active use, and a popular choice for decorating wearables and kitchen linens. After all, it literally was the only color able to take the heat! Within a few years, outline and decorative embroidery done on a white or muslin background became known as *redwork*.

By the 1880s, when silk embroidered Crazy quilts became wildly popular, redwork was a 'little sister' trend. It used the same motif designs and general stitches as the Crazy, but in a much easier outline-embroidered form, accented by other stitching on the seamlines. More colorfast dyes were introduced in the early 1880s, and soon "redwork" was also shaded blue, brown, pink, gold, even cream! (Technically, the title remains the same – so these are *blue* redwork, *green* redwork, and so on.)

Redwork-style embroidered quilts remained popular past World War I, when they began to incorporate windmills, Dutch children in wooden shoes and other motifs, brought back by returning soldiers from their experience overseas. ('Delft' blue – actually a teal – was often

**GIRLS OF THE GOLDEN WEST** *block detail (redwork version), 2009, made by Bonnie DeVries and Cindy Brick. Baby Doe Tabor takes the stage in this redwork-style embroidered block; she could just as easily be done in pink and white, brown and white… or perennially popular Turkey red and white.*

Baby Doe Tabor

used for these Holland-themed redwork quilts.) By World War II, multi-colored embroidery was gaining popularity, not only in quilts but dresser scarves, tablecloths and other decorative linens.

Children learned how to stitch by making redwork squares; at one point, a stamped square cost a penny, giving it another name, the *penny square*. (These blocks were also used to keep sick children quiet during the early 20th century's flu epidemics – then lost to the flames when anything connected to the recovering patient was burned.)

Redwork designs were everywhere: for sale in catalogs and dry goods stores, free in magazines…even traced from magazine and newspaper advertisements! They were also available as souvenirs from world fairs

## The History of Redwork CONT.

and other cultural events – one series of redwork patterns commemorated the buildings of the Pan American Exposition in Buffalo, NY – and the assassination of President McKinley, when he visited there in September, 1901.

Motifs included farm animals, flowers, children, popular events, angels, phrases (like "Good Morning" and "Good Night"), famous people, Orient-themed parasols, fans, even odd things like talking owls and bugs. (The spiderweb began its popular reign here, as a symbol of luck and good fortune.) Whatever could be copied or drawn was popular on a redwork quilt. Blocks were usually stitched, using muslin – cloth feedsacks were a popular choice – then the block joins themselves embroidered, usually with more difficult stitches, like herringbone or feather. Sometimes stitches were combined for a more elaborate look.

Redwork has re-emerged today as a popular technique. We still love it in Turkey Red, although generally any color is colorfast! To learn more about this appealing style, visit my 2008 book, *Crazy Quilts* (Voyageur Press), or Deborah Harding's comprehensive two-volume *Red and White* (Rizzoli, 2000).

# EMBROIDERY STITCH GLOSSARY

In America's earliest days, one's skill with embroidery and other stitching was thought to measure one's ultimate worth as a woman! Young girls not only learned embroidery at their mother's knee – but if they were lucky enough to go to school, at the academy. This attitude persisted into the early 20th century, when increased opportunities for women in previously closed fields gave them less time for "womanly" pursuits.

If your mother (or in this author's case, her grandmother) didn't teach you how to embroider, don't lose hope. Dorothy Bond's excellent guide, *Crazy Quilt Stitches* (see Sources on page 128), shows how to do the basic stitching – and combine stitches for exciting new combinations. Her diagrams here will help you get started. Use an embroidery needle (I also like a big-eyed quilting needle), plus a skein of embroidery floss. Each 'rope' of floss unravels into multiple strands; you need two for most work, but just one for finer details.

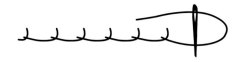

**Buttonhole Stitch**

**Chain Stitch**

**Stem (or outline) Stitch**

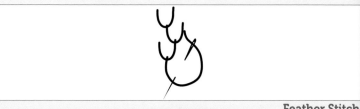

**Feather Stitch**

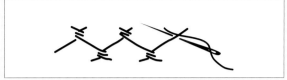
**Herringbone Stitch**

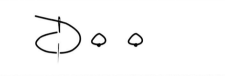
**Lazy Daisy Stitch**

**Sheaf Stitch**

**Herringbone/Lazy Daisy combo**

Your primary tool in redwork is the stem, or outline stitch. Practice, using a scrap of extra fabric and two strands of floss, before you begin one of the Golden West Ladies. (You'll also want to try the redwork stitcher's other primary weapons, Feather and Herringbone, if you'd like to embroider on seamlines elsewhere in the quilt.) The stem stitch is also known as the Kensington stitch, after a charitable institution sponsored by Queen Victoria, meant to benefit impoverished young gentle-women. Socialites would leave commissions for quilts, pillows, curtains and other decorative items – and this needlework would then keep the young women from starvation. (Or acting, which was much worse!)

Other versions of the Kensington stitch are the split stitch, and a long/short stitch combination used to fill in areas. (We see the latter today more in crewel and woolwork.) It seems ironic, though, that one of the easiest stitches in the needleworkers' repertoire is also named for a group that was supposed to feature superior work!

*All stitch diagrams used with permission from Dorothy Bond's* Crazy Quilt Stitches.

# THE HISTORY OF THE SEWING MACHINE

Sewing-type machines have a much longer history than you would think. The first patent, for an embroidery machine with an eye-pointed needle (an essential for today's machine), appeared in 1750, courtesy of Charles Weisenthal, a German mechanic who lived in London. Four decades later, an English cabinetmaker named Thomas Saint applied for a patent for a machine for "stitching, quilting & sewing."

It wasn't until 1831, though, that a poor tailor named Barthelemy Thimmonier produced a machine that worked... sort of. It may have been heavy and clunky, but within a few years, 80 seamstresses were sewing uniforms for the French military, at 100 stitches a minute.

Another machine appeared in 1845, this one by an American. Noted the *Scientific American*, in its September 1846 issue: "We have heretofore noticed the extraordinary invention by Mr. Elias Howe, Jr. of Cambridge, MA – a machine that sews beautiful and strong seams in cloth as rapid as nine tailors." Howe's main problem was lack of funds – few could afford his beautiful machine, and he was eventually forced to pawn it after a trip to England, in order to return home.

Other inventors added their contributions, including Walter Hunt, inventor of the safety pin. But another machine appeared in 1850, from a failed actor and success-ful inventor, Isaac Singer, along with his partners Phelps and Zieber. Singer invented only two of the ten aspects needed for his sewing machine, and 'borrowed' the rest. But his was one of the first machines to sew consistently.

Sewing machine sales were slow at first. In 1851, one of Singer's machines cost $100, a sum few could afford. Even a pay-by-the-month plan conceived by Singer's partner, Edward Clark, in 1856, only bumped sales a little. Sewing machines were sent via the Isthmus of Panama to Chile... and California...by the mid-1860s. The Civil War's end eased funds; the railroad's completion eased transportation; and the role of the sewing machine in the West began to grow.

**Curious to know more?** Read *Singer and the Sewing Machine* by Ruth Brandon.

# HOW TO MAKE GIRLS OF THE GOLDEN WEST, REDWORK-STYLE

**FINISHED QUILT SIZE: 56" X 56" (3 ROWS OF 3 – 13" BLOCKS, ON POINT, PLUS AN OUTER 2" BORDER)**

## FABRIC AND EMBROIDERY REQUIREMENTS

Cobalt blue cotton embroidery floss: 1 1/2 skeins per block, for a total of 14 skeins.

Cobalt blue solid (pieced triangle squares): 1 1/2 yards

White solid (pieced triangle squares, rest of the quilt): 4 yards

Backing: 4 yards (cut 2 panels 30" x 59" and join vertically)

Batting: 64" x 64" square

Binding: 2/3 yard (use white if you want the binding to blend in – blue if you prefer a strong contrast and framing effect)

## CUTTING REQUIREMENTS

### Blocks

**Pieced Blocks** (9 – 13" pieced blocks needed)

Read through the entire instructions before you start cutting. Decide whether you'd like to cut your triangles square by square (*Triangle Rule #1*, page 45) or using the quick-pieced method (pages 33 and 53). **Please note:** this top uses a "floating" edge (see page 42) trimmed to fit the outer pieced triangle border.

*Block Centers:* Embroider the 9 ladies on the cream fabric, leaving at least 2" extra all around. Center and cut each out as a 6 1/2" square (9 total).

*Pieced inner and outer 1" block borders:* From cobalt blue solid, cut 2" squares – 18 per block, for a total of 162 squares. Cut the squares in half diagonally, (Triangle Rule #1, page 45), for a total of 324 triangles. If you use the quick-pieced method instead, you need 17 sheets, with leftovers (see page 53).

You need to cut the same amount of squares (and eventually triangles) from the white as you did for the cobalt blue... unless you're using the quick-pieced method. Before you do the triangle squares, though– cut the larger squares and triangles first. Begin with:

*Alternating Blocks, Large Setting Triangles and Corner Triangles* (4 – 13" finished blocks, 8 large setting triangles and 4 corner triangles needed):

From white solid, cut 2 – 18" squares, then cut these diagonally twice for 8 large setting triangles. (See the Triangle Rules #2 insert on page 45 for help.) Next cut 4 – 13" squares. Finally, cut 2 – 9 1/2" squares diagonally once for 4 corner triangles.

*Outer Pieced Triangle Quilt Border (2"):*
From white solid, cut 3" squares – 66 total – then cut each diagonally for 112 triangles.

From cobalt blue solid, also cut 3" squares – also 66 total, then cut again diagonally for 112 triangles.

(You need an equal amount of cobalt blue triangles. Use Triangle Rule #1, page 45. Or quick-piece your triangle square blocks, using the grid on page 53— enlarge it 200%.) Back to the Pieced Blocks:

*Inner block setting triangles:* From the rest of the white solid, cut a 8 1/4" square diagonally both ways to yield 4 triangles. (See the Triangle Rules #2 on page 45 for help.) You need 9 – 8 1/4" squares, for a total of 36 triangles.

Also, for the *outer block border 1" accent squares,* cut 4 – 1 1/2" squares for each block, for a total of 36 squares.

Block Diagram,
redwork version,
finished size 13"

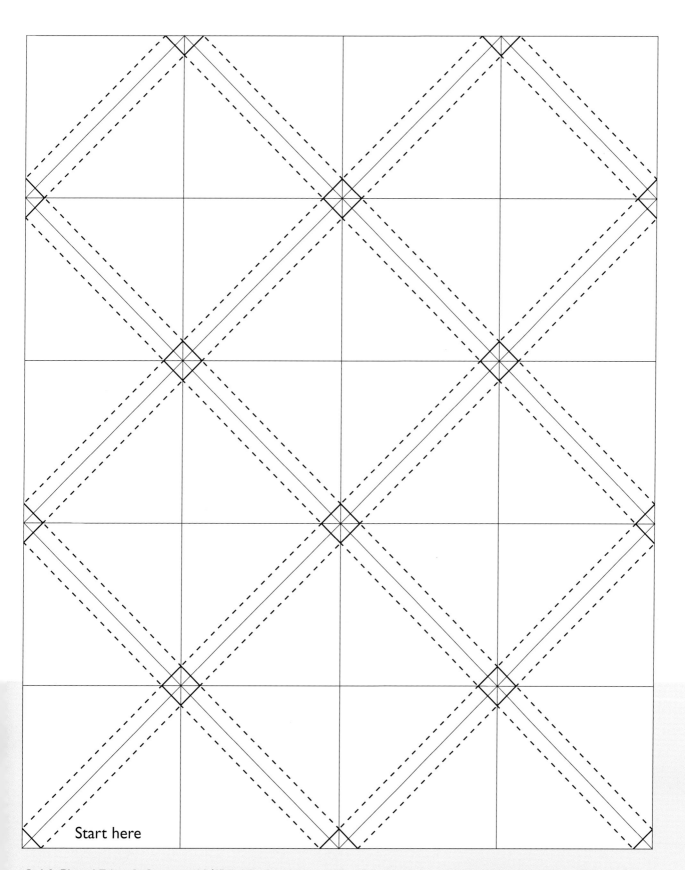

Start here

Quick-Pieced Triangle Square grid (1" finished squares -= 40 - 1" finished pieced triangle squares. Note: This grid should measure 7" x 8 3/4" after scanning or photocopying. See page 33 for a description of this method – it may be substituted for cutting the triangles individually or in pairs (squares). Note: sew on dotted lines.

# Backing, Batting and Binding

See General Instructions on page 36.

# Block Assembly

### PIECED BLOCKS (13" FINISHED):

Follow the general block instructions on the scrappy Girls of the Golden West version (see pages 41-43) – but substitute cobalt blue and white for the fabric scraps and muslin in the inner and outer pieced block borders. Sew 1 blue triangle to 1 white for a pieced triangle square; repeat until you have enough for the blocks. **Check**: do your triangle squares measure 1 1/2"? If not, trim to size.

Using an embroidered Lady 6 1/2" center square, and the blue/white pieced triangle units, put your block together, section by section until it's done. (Substitute the white accent squares for the California Gold squares used in the outer block border.)

Make a total of 9 blocks – each one featuring a different Lady.

### Outer Pieced Triangle Border:

*(Yes, this is different from the other scrappy quilt)*

From the cut triangles (originally 3" squares), sew 1 blue to 1 white to make a pieced triangle square; you need a total of 116 triangles each of cobalt blue and white. **Check**: do your triangle squares measure 2 1/2"? If not, trim to size. Stitch 30 of these together for a border row; repeat, for 2 rows total. Then stitch 29 together for a border row; repeat, for 2 rows total. Press, then set aside border rows for now.

# Quilt Assembly

### STITCHING THE TOP

Follow the lead of the general instructions for the scrappy Girls of the Golden West to lay out and piece the top. (**Note:** This top, like the tip on page 42, is designed to "float.") Double-check after pressing: does the top measure 56 1/2" square? That's the quilt size you need to fit on the outer border; trim to size, if needed. (See the first pattern's tips on "floating" for extra help.)

**Outer Border:** Fit and match edges of the 2 shorter rows on the top and bottom of the quilt – one per side. Stitch in place, taking care of make the triangle points crisp. Fit, match and stitch the other 2 sides to finish the quilt top.

# Finishing the Top

**Note:** Many redwork quilts were never quilted; instead they were tied, or simply underlined with another sheet for a summer spread. If you like that flat, old-fashioned look, you may even decide to omit the batting!

The scrappy version features a Wild Rose quilting motif, done in full and partial versions. (See the next page for the Assembly Diagram – and page 44 for the Wild Rose motif.) If you like that look, you may want to embroider the Wild Rose motifs on, rather than quilt them. Follow the general instructions on the scrappy version for each, and the embroidery stitch glossary for stitching help. (Be sure to add 1 1/2 skeins of cobalt blue floss for every wild rose motif you stitch, full or partial.)

Layer your top with batting and backing (or no batting); baste. If you're planning to quilt the top, use cream thread. Use the quilting suggestions in the scrappy Girls version on page 44– or outline quilt sparingly. Bind to finish the quilt.

Redwork Style Assembly Diagram

# BABY DOE TABOR

1854 - 1935
THE
MATCHLESS
GIRL

ELIZABETH
BONDUEL
MCCOURT
DOE TABOR

Lizzie McCourt Doe, nicknamed "Baby" by passerby who admired her striking good looks, was the discontented wife of a miner gone bust – until she met a new silver millionaire named Horace Tabor. Horace, who ran a grocery store and post office with his sensible wife Augusta, had grubstaked many miners until two men named Hook and Rische came along. Their mine, the Little Pittsburg, paid off... and Horace was rich.

Then Baby Doe came along. After (secret) quickie divorces for both Horace and Elizabeth, a (secret) civil wedding and a lavish 1883 public wedding in Washington, D.C. (President Arthur even attended), Baby Doe and her husband had two daughters in quick succession, and lived in a Denver mansion with classical statues out front. ('Naked!' said the neighbors.) No one came to call on this beautiful upstart, though she was furtively watched while sitting in the reserved Tabor box at the theatre (name trimmed in silver from their Matchless Mine).

Within a decade, silver prices plunged when the Silver Standard was devalued. Horace, along with many others whose fortunes were based on silver, found himself painfully short of cash. He mortgaged his few valuable properties in an effort to save the others – and lost everything, instead. Horace and Baby, along with their young daughters, moved to a small cottage in Denver. (Augusta, in contrast, carefully preserved her wealth after her divorce, and died, still loving her Tabor, in California.)

Horace became postmaster of Denver and died of appendicitis soon after in 1899. On his deathbed, he supposedly told Baby, "Hang onto the Matchless." She took him literally and moved to a small caretaker's cabin near the mine, its tunnels now filled with water, near Leadville, CO.

Though still young and beautiful, Lizzie Tabor spurned all male companionship; her main interests lay in re-opening the Matchless, and raising her daughters. But the heyday of silver mining was over. One child soon left for Wisconsin; the other led a wild life and eventually died, scalded to death, in Chicago. (Baby always said that her reckless Silver actually went into a convent...though she knew better.) Baby walked the streets in rusty black accented by a wooden cross and rosary of binder twine, her feet in old miner's boots. She died an old woman in 1935, frozen to death in her little cabin during a blizzard.

## Baby Doe's Quilt

An intricately made Crazy quilt resides at the Frontier Historical Society in Glenwood Springs, CO, stitched with ribbons and scraps from Baby Doe Tabor's dresses. The quilt is said to have been made by Bertha Delker, who made dresses for many of Leadville's wealthy ladies. Baby Doe cared little for convention, and her needlework skills were well-known. Could she have contributed a stitch or two to her dressmaker's beautiful Crazy quilt?

## COULD BABY DOE HAVE HIDDEN IT?

*Specific info is vague, but Karl Von Mueller records a 100-ounce gold cache discovered near the mine hoist by Baby Doe's cabin, sometime between her death and 1979.*
- *Treasure Hunter's Manual #7*

Baby Doe Tabor

Margaret ("Maggie") Tobin Brown was headed up in life. She'd gotten a job in a tobacco factory near her home in Hannibal, MO, then moved to Colorado, where she caught the eye of Johnny Brown, the manager of a gold mine. Johnny helped secure another fabulously rich mine for his company, and was rewarded with a large chunk of valuable stock. The Brown family moved to Denver, where their downtown mansion, not far from the state capitol, was guarded by stone lions on the front steps. Maggie enjoyed travel, fancy decorating and fancier living with her friends, including singers, actresses and European royalty.

Her husband preferred cigars, the outdoors and the rough comforts of his Leadville friends…and soon Maggie and J.J. parted. (They never divorced, though they lived separately to the end of their lives.) Maggie continued to travel, study and learn new languages. While in Europe in April 1912, she received word that her grandson was desperately sick. Maggie took the fastest route home – the maiden voyage of the luxury liner Titanic. When it sank, she commandeered LifeBoat No. 6, the boat she and other society ladies were put in and spent the rest of the night singing, talking and urging the others to row. (She did a good share of it herself, as well.) When Maggie finally landed in New York City, she began fundraising for

# MOLLY BROWN

## 1867-1932

## THE

## UNSINKABLE

## MARGARET

## TOBIN BROWN

second and third-class passengers who had lost everything. (She also found out that her grandson had recovered.) When asked why she hadn't gone down with the boat, she is reported to have said, "Typical Brown luck. We're unsinkable!"

There are many stories about Maggie: she was called "Molly" (never in her lifetime)...she grew up with Mark Twain (his family, yes – Samuel Clemens, no)...she accidentally burned a huge amount of cash in a stove (not true)...she was crude, and Denver society shunned her. (Actually Mrs. Crawford Hill, the self-acknowledged head of Denver's "Sacred 36," gave a reception

celebrating Maggie's rescue from the Titanic. Thank Debbie Reynolds and the popular 1964 movie, *The Unsinkable Molly Brown,* for many of these interesting statements.) Maggie's income gradually dwindled, especially after J.J.'s death in 1922. Toward the end of her life, she became an actress. She died in her sleep in New York City's Barbizon, a hotel for actresses publicized in the movie *Stage Door.* The autopsy revealed Maggie's final surprise: an inoperable brain tumor.

**One of Margaret Brown's greatest achievements** is rarely mentioned today: along with a Denver judge, Ben Lindsey, she was the first to urge that juveniles be tried –and housed – separately from adults and the standard prisons. The first juvenile court system was established soon after.

# NANCY KELSEY

## 1823-1896

### FIRST WOMAN WEST INTO CALIFORNIA

NANCY ROBERTS KELSEY

**Nancy Kelsey** not only was the first documented Caucasian woman to visit Utah, but she was also the first to cross the Sierra Nevadas – thanks in great part to her restless husband Ben, who wanted to head west. The Kelseys, along with several members of their extended family and others, formed the Bartleson-Bidwell Company – the first organized wagon train to head west for California.

They were lured in part by John Marsh, a schoolteacher who had wandered into California in 1836 and began practicing medicine, using skills he picked up from an Army surgeon. Marsh's letters to various newspapers urged others to join him; eventually the Western Emigration Society recruited 500 people who signed pledges, "armed and equipped to cross the Rocky Mountains to California."

The year was 1841, and the Oregon Trail was still fairly new. More than 60 people started the trip from a sapling grove near Weston, MO; one of them, a young schoolteacher named John Bidwell, kept a journal. His entries that follow often give us the best picture of Nancy at this period in her life.

The party's guide, at least as far as Idaho, was Thomas "Broken-Hand" Fitzpatrick, a famous mountain man who knew the western expanses well. After that, they were on their own. The group, eventually worn down to 32 men and one women, spent seven long months on the trail, first in heavily loaded wagons, then discarding items as they went. As time went on, possessions were cut to the bare minimum, or consolidated with others. Wagons were abandoned as oxen died or were stolen by the Indiana. To save wear and tear on their own oxen, Nancy, who turned 18 while on the trip, walked barefoot most of the way, her baby daughter Martha Ann in her arms. They finally arrived in early November at John Marsh's ranch "with no guide, no compass, nothing but the sun to direct them." He greeted them with less than enthusiasm. By November 25, they'd reached Sutter's Fort.

The Kelseys never stayed anywhere for long. The family would settle into a new place until Ben grew restless and wanted to move on. Nancy's life was spent this way, often in rough country and hardship, until Ben died in Los Angeles. She then moved to the Cuyama Valley in Santa Barbara County, California and eventually died there. Her last request was to be buried in a store-bought coffin. It took a while, including boxing the coffin in a larger wooden box and hauling it from Santa Barbara, but Nancy eventually got her wish.

## The Betsy Ross of California

In June 1846, a group of American settlers raised a new flag over the plaza at Sonoma, California, symbolizing their independence from Mexico. Unfortunately, Mexico didn't agree; California had been split up into large land grants that were used, among other things, to run cattle. The 'new' Californians weren't rescued until 24 days later, when the U.S. Navy sailed into Monterey on July 7 and raised the U.S. flag, claiming California for its own. (A number of the settlers, who didn't like this new development any more than interference from the Mexicans, were promptly jailed.)

Who made this new Bear Revolt flag? None other than Nancy Kelsey, using unbleached cotton, a strip of red flannel from her petticoat and berry juice to ink the proud words "**California Republic**".

"Where my husband goes, I can go. I can better stand the hardships of the journey than the anxieties for an absent husband."

—*Nancy Kelsey*

# LOTTA CRABTREE

## 1847-1924

### CHARLOTTE MIGNON CRABTREE

Miss Lotta. The California Diamond. The San Francisco Favorite...otherwise known as Lotta Crabtree. This feisty little performer grew up performing across the west in gold camps, doing Irish jigs and singing popular ditties. The Eternal Child, as the *New York Times* called her, was one of the best-known actresses of the "Gold Coast."

Born in New York City of Irish parents John and Mary Ann, Lotta and her mother headed to San Francisco to reunite with John Crabtree, a bookseller who'd gone west to seek his fortune. John didn't bother to meet them. Fortunately, Mary Ann had friends to stay with; when John finally did appear, he brought his family to Grass Valley, CA, where Mary Ann started a boardinghouse.

One of the Crabtrees' neighbors was Lola Montez, a notorious actress and hootchy cootchy dancer. She took an interest in the young Lotta, teaching her how to dance and sing. Soon after, Lotta was 'borrowed' by a local impresario, who took her to a local mining camp. She was an immediate hit; the miners cheered, and pelted her with gold nuggets and coins. The promoter made a business proposal to Mary Ann, and the family began touring camps in Nevada and California, where Lotta would perform. Mary Ann would gather up the money, and store it in an old carpetbag. Mary Ann also invested shrewdly in real estate and bonds.

Eventually, Lotta began touring the East Coast with her own theatrical company, starring in comedic roles. By this time, she was also called "The Nation's Darling." She had taken to sprinkling cayenne pepper in her red hair, smoking thin black cigars, and wearing her skirts shorter, to show off her ankles as she danced. As usual, Lotta's mother collected the money, and shielded her daughter from bad influences (like boys).

Miss Lotta never married. After her mother's death in 1905, she stayed with her friends, traveled and enjoyed driving ponies and painting. She purchased the Brewster Hotel in Boston, and began living there. By her death in 1924, Lotta's Gold Rush fortune had grown to a comfortable $4 million...which went to charities for actors, veterans and animals.

# LOTTA'S FOUNTAIN

Lotta's concern for animals was legendary. Decades after she'd moved east, Lotta commissioned a metal fountain in Philadelphia, had it shipped west, then donated it to San Francisco. "Lotta's Fountain" was set up on Market Street, not far from the newest and most elegant hotels. For decades it served its purpose for thirsty dogs, cats and horses, among others.

Then came 1906 – and the Great Earthquake. Brick and stone buildings collapsed; wood ones burned. Practically the only thing left standing was Lotta's Fountain. People gathered there daily to check reports on the missing, and post messages to their loved ones. For some weeks, the main "post office" was the fountain, until life slowly began to resume. San Franciscans never forgot. To this day, people gather every year in front of Lotta's Fountain, now restored to its original beauty, on April 18, the anniversary of the quake.

# LOTTA CRABTREE

## 1847-1924

### CHARLOTTE MIGNON CRABTREE

Lotta toured the East Coast with her own theatrical company, starring in comedic roles. Called "The Nation's Darling," she had taken to sprinkling cayenne pepper in her red hair to make it sparkle under the light, smoking thin black cigars, and wearing her skirts shorter, to show off her ankles as she danced.

# BELLE STARR

**1848-1889**

**BANDIT QUEEN OF THE PLAINS**

**MYRA MAYBELLE SHIRLEY REED STARR (ACTUALLY STARR TWICE: SHE MARRIED TWO BROTHERS)**

### Desperado...or just misunderstood?

Belle Starr's life is a puzzle. Did she lead a band of outlaws, robbing, shooting and cattle rustling? Or was she just a horse thief who happened to be in the wrong place at the wrong time?

Myra Belle grew up the daughter of a well-to-do saloonkeeper in Carthage, MO. Although she was genteelly educated in at the local women's academy (founded by her father), she enjoyed riding with her older brother Bud and his friends more. They taught her to shoot and handle her weapons, and she spent many happy hours with them. (Those childhood friends – including Jesse and Frank James, and their fellow gang member, Cole Younger – would often stop by Belle's house in adulthood for a meal and a place to stay.)

The Civil War changed everything. Belle's brother joined the Confederate side, and along with his friends, became part of Quantrill Raiders, a guerrilla group with a fearsome reputation for burning and looting. Belle was forced to move south with her parents after their property in Carthage was destroyed.

Belle married her childhood crush, Jim Reed, moved to Texas (she soon came back to Missouri), and had a daughter she called Pearl. But all was not well. Jim was involved in some unsavory activities, and died during a gunfight. If Belle wasn't involved with shady activities by this point, that soon changed. She married one of their friends, Sam Starr, and moved to Indian Territory. (Sam, as part-Cherokee, had the right to live and own land there.) Soon she was actively helping out with Sam's work, including horse stealing and passing counterfeit money. If people stopped by, it was only neighborly to offer them...and their friends...a place for the night. No matter if a posse was not on their trail – everyone was welcome at the Starrs.

Belle kept up her favorite activities. She played the piano at her small cabin on Younger's Bend – at a time when that piano was probably the only one for many miles. She kept a shelf of books, as well, did target practice (she was an excellent shot) and enjoyed horseback rides around the countryside. Belle wore a favorite black velvet riding habit, hat with plume (shown in her portrait), and kept gunbelts strapped loosely over her lap. Two pearl-handled revolvers, a gift from her friend Cole Younger, completed the ensemble.

By the time Belle's daughter, as well as a son, were grown, she and Sam had both served time in prison – Belle in Detroit for passing bad money. Sam was dead, shot in a brawl. (You lose more husbands that way!) And Belle was on the lookout for another husband. She found him in Sam's little brother. The marriage wasn't happy, but it allowed her to stay on in Indian Territory.

In 1889, Belle was murdered, shot off her horse as she left a neighbor's house, chewing on a piece of cornbread. (To this day, no one knows who did it, but suspects include a disgruntled neighbor, Belle's son – and her husband.) She was buried in her riding habit, best jewelry, and with her favorite guns tucked in her hands. (Someone robbed her grave soon after, stealing both jewelry and guns.) Within six months, July Starr, Belle's newest husband, was also dead – shot in a gunfight, like his predecessors.

Not long after, the dime novel *Bella Starr, the Bandit Queen, or the Female Jesse James,* was published, by a man who had never met Belle or talked to her friends. The woman who may have been nothing more than a small-time horse thief soon was the "Petticoat Terror of the Plains" and a bandit queen. Did she really have her own gang? Was she the crimelord the novels made her out to be? At least we know one thing; she had bad taste in friends and husbands.

# BELLE STARR'S IRON DOOR CACHE

About 1881, so the story goes, Belle headed up a band of cutthroats whose specialty was robbing stagecoaches or trains. One of their most productive heists was a train, which just happened to be carrying the Denver Mint's latest shipment of government gold. After the bandits lugged off the heavy bags, Belle realized they wouldn't get far, carrying such weight. So she ordered one of the men to pull off one of the railroad car's heavy sliding doors, using horses. The band headed into the rough country of the Wichita Mountains in Oklahoma, dragging the door. They found a cave, stashed the moneybags inside, then fixed the heavy iron door in place over the entrance, securing it with a heavy padlock, just in case. Then they scattered.

A second robbery went wrong, and most of the gang was killed. After Belle's murder in 1889, few existed who knew about the robbery – and the gold.

This would have been considered just another fancy tale of lost treasure...but a heavy iron door has been repeatedly seen in a remote canyon of the Wichitas, up a slope near the canyon wall, mostly covered by brush and rocks. It can only be noticed when the sunlight hits it in a certain way, close to dusk. Discoverers range from hikers to farmers traveling through; some knew the story about the treasure and attempted to open the door, but it was rusted shut. When they tried to return with better equipment, they couldn't find the right canyon – or just the right spot. An older lady from Missouri showed up in town, carrying a key she said would unlock the door. (It was given to her by a bandit she'd nursed during his last sickness, she said.) Unfortunately, the lady couldn't find the door, either.

Does the iron door hide fabulous riches? You'll have to look for it yourself. Start at the Wichita Wildlife Refuge, near Indiahoma, then take a shortcut skirting Elk Mountain. The rusted iron door is in a deep canyon somewhere north of Treasure Lake. Be there at sunset; that's when it's seen to best advantage, say its viewers.

*Buried Treasures of the American Southwest*

An image of Belle's favorite mare was engraved on her headstone, along with these words:

Shed not for her the bitter tear,

Nor give the heart to vain regret

Tis but the casket that lies here,

The gem that filled it sparkles yet.

# FERMINIA SARRAS

**1840-1915**

**COPPER BARONESS**

**FERMINIA (OR FERMINA) SARRAS (OR SARARIS, SERARAS, SARAREZ)**

**The lady who arrived in Esmeralda County, Nevada around 1881 was a puzzle.** She described herself as "a Spanish lady of royal blood," a descendant of the Contreras family of Nicaragua whose ancestor, Roderigo de Contreras, ruled during the 16th century. (The county's tax records list her simply as "Spanish lady, Belleville.")

Ferminia came to Nevada with her husband Pablo Flores and their four daughters: Conchetta, Conception, Juanita and Emma. The two youngest daughters were left at the Nevada Orphans Asylum in Virginia City (for safety, or so Ferminia may have reasoned), and the rest of the family headed for the mining camps of Belleville and Candelaria. Ferminia seems to have worked alongside her husband, something many women did not do.

Apparently, it wasn't enough for Pablo. He went his own way, and eventually Ferminia married at least five times, to Archie McCormack, Fermine Arriga and others. She also had a son, Joseph Marshall, though she was not married to anyone named Marshall at the time. Ferminia preferred younger men for many of her relationships: Archie McCormack, one of her husbands, was 12 years younger than she was. Archie was also good with a gun – another skill Ferminia especially valued, since it helped protect her various properties. (Archie was eventually killed in a gun battle, an all-too-common fate in mining camps those days.)

Many people thought that Ferminia was a Mexican or Spanish princess, something she seems to have met with amusement, but didn't bother to refute. What is clear: she benefitted from her associations to places further south. Mexico and other countries allowed a woman to own her own property, and control her own estate – a privilege rarely given to Caucasian women who were American citizens.

And Ferminia owned several valuable properties. She worked them with her children, or her current companion. As early as 1883, she was prospecting in Candelaria; she filed on several copper claims in the Santa Fe District, then moved on to Silver Peak, though she didn't have much luck there. Eventually, she moved back to the Santa

Fe district in 1899, where she prospected alone, wearing pants, boots and a backpack.

By the time she died in 1915, Ferminia had found – and sold – several successful copper mining claims, named after her family, friends and lovers. She spent much of her profits on luxurious trips to San Francisco, staying at fancy hotels and eating well, in the company of her latest admirer. When her money ran out, she would return home to prospect some more. Any leftover gold coins were stashed in outbuildings on her property. Banks weren't safe – who would look in a chicken coop, anyways?

Although Ferminia lived in several places, she stayed mostly at Luning, NV. Later on, the town of Mina was named in her honor. Several valuable mines in the Giroux Canyon area of Nevada are still being mined today, thanks to the proud "Nevada Copper Queen" who originally discovered them.

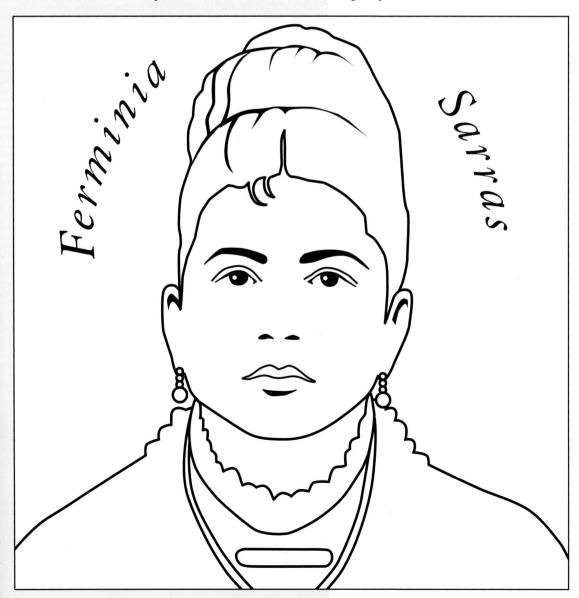

# MARIE PANTALON

**1824 (OR 1815) – 1892**

**GRAPE-LOVER, GOLD-DIGGER**

**JEANNE MARIE SUIZE (OR SUISE)**

**Marie Suize** was born in Thone, France (some accounts say "the mountains of Savoie"), but grew up on the streets of Paris. It was a rough and tumble life, with few opportunities. When news of California's gold strikes arrived in Europe, Marie's brother saw this as his golden opportunity. So did Marie.

The two arrived in San Francisco in early 1850, after somehow scraping together money for ship's passage. Originally, Marie had thought to get a high-paying job as a maid...or so she told her brother. Instead, they both headed for the gold camps. Marie found, though, that the long dresses she wore would drag and scrape in the mud as she worked. Why not be more comfortable, and borrow (horror of horrors) her brother's pants, instead?

So Marie Pantalon, or Madame Trousers, was born. Although she reverted back to dresses whenever she moved back to more genteel society, Marie much preferred wearing the heavy pants of the day. A German-American dry goods peddler named Levi Strauss was selling a heavy canvas trouser with extra pockets to hold ore, designed by his partner, a tailor named Jacob Davis. No doubt Marie bought some of these *blue jeans*, too.

Miners had never seen women in pants. What was this upstart Frenchwoman doing? Marie took more than her share of abuse about it; she was even arrested for indecent behavior! But she beat the charges, and eventually her odd behavior was accepted.

Marie had another secret: a gold claim that was producing nicely. She lived with the fear that someone else would attempt to jump her claim – a danger that was all too common in mining country, let alone for a woman. How could she protect herself? Marie planted a vineyard on her land, to hide any evidence of mining activity. The grapes flourished, and so did the gold.

Eventually, this enterprising woman became one of California's first brandy merchants. She opened a wine shop in San Francisco, which did well for decades, and continued to prospect for gold whenever she could. As far as we know, she never married or had children. But she continued to insist on wearing trousers whenever possible.

Marie died an old woman, and was buried in an unmarked grave in Jackson, California's cemetery – the Catholic section. More than a century later, the towns of Jackson and Thone paid for a commemorative head-stone in her honor. No photos of Marie are known, so this drawing of her is a guess...but Marie Pantalon took obstacles and remade them into unique opportunities.

"We saw last April, a French woman, standing in Angel's Creek, dipping and pouring water into the washer, which her husband [probably her brother] was rocking. She wore short boots, white duck pantaloons, a red flannel shirt, with a black leather belt and a Panama hat. Day after day she could be seen working quietly and steadily, performing her share of the gold digging labor."

-*San Francisco* Daily Alta
Goldrush.com

# YELLOW ROSE OF TEXAS

## C.1800? (1815?) - ??
## HEROINE OF THE BATTLE OF SAN JACINTO - APRIL 21, 1836

### EMILY D. WEST, NEE MORGAN

**The Language of Flowers**
is an ancient theory that assigns
every growing thing has a specific
meaning — good or bad. Our
ancestors knew it well, having learned
it in school and popular use. What's
the yellow rose's meaning? Suspicion
and betrayal! (It changed to
"friendship" in the 20th century,
thanks in part to florist's associations.)
For more, see my book
*Stitcher's Language of Flowers*.

James Morgan's bustling settlement was located near the mouth of the San Jacinto River. Flatboats loaded with supplies pushed off for Houston from Morgan's Point. And the prettiest, smartest woman in the area was Emily West.

We're not sure exactly what she looked like. Some accounts say that she was a "winsome light-skinned slave of James Morgan." Or she may have been an indentured servant, originally from Bermuda, who came with Morgan when he moved from New York. (Slaves and indentured servants took their master's last name, and Emily is often referred to as "Morgan.") Other accounts insist that Emily was actually a free African-American born in New Haven, CT, who signed on for a year as a housekeeper for New Washington's hotel, and arrived in New Washington, TX via schooner in December, 1835.

Emily's moniker as "yellow" gives us a clue – this, also "high yellow," was a popular way in the early 19th century to describe a person of mixed black and white blood. Whatever her racial makeup, Emily found herself in the middle of a political storm by April 1836. The Texans were smack in the middle of a war for their independence with Mexico – and losing badly. The Battle of the Alamo, fought only a month earlier, was a raw memory, and the Texan army was hounded by Mexican soldiers and their commander, Antonio Lopez de Santa Anna.

Emily's boss, James Morgan, had left for Galveston to command Fort Travis, leaving, say some accounts, Emily in charge. When Santa Anna marched into town, his eye fell on Emily...and he resolved to enjoy her charms forthwith. In spite of his generals' protests, the Mexican army was ordered to set up camp. Meanwhile, Emily sent word to Sam Houston, the commander of the Texans, to hurry back.

Early next morning, the Texans attacked the sleeping camp. In less than an hour, it was over. The Mexican army had been routed. Santa Anna was captured while trying to escape, literally with his pants down, while Emily was cooking his breakfast. It was a decisive victory for Texas: the Battle of San Jacinto.

Emily left Texas in 1837, probably for New York. Some accounts have her granted freedom by her master; others say she regained her 'free papers,' lost at the battle site, and had passage home arranged by Morgan. She disappears soon after. But proud Texans have never forgotten the beautiful woman who patriotically gave up her virtue for their republic. And the *"Yellow Rose of Texas"* has reigned ever since in their hearts.

"Yellow Rose of Texas" has long been a favored title for Texan First Ladies, regardless of their background.

Begin in the center by making several French-knots.

Work a loose stem-stitch, forming loops which stand up slightly.

Lengthen and flatten stitch on outer edge.

**Rambler Rose**

**Rambler Rose variation (with feather stitch)**

*- Courtesy of Dorothy Bond and her book, Crazy Quilt Stitches*

Western TV shows picture women with their long hair down. In reality, women of marriageable age kept their hair "up" and parted in the middle. Back hair was braided or coiled into a bun; front hair arranged in soft waves called bandeaux. (Bangs were not popular until later in the century.) Women only washed their hair a few times during the year, and often dressed their heads with extra pomade to get the flat, oiled look so admired.

Emily's yellow rose is thought to be Harison's Yellow Rose, a hardy rugosa type still grown out west. Pioneers carried cuttings stuck in a potato – a method that works surprisingly well. Order your own plant from High Country Roses; see www.highcountryroses.com (or Sources on page 128).

There's a yellow rose in Texas
That I am a going to see
No other darky knows her
No one only me

She cried so when I left her
It like to broke my heart
And if I ever find her
We nevermore will part

She's the sweetest rose of color
This darky ever knew
Her eyes are bright as diamonds
They sparkle like the dew

You may talk about dearest May
and sing of Rosa Lee
But the yellow rose of Texas
Beats the belles of Tennessee

Lyrics from earliest copy of *"Yellow Rose of Texas,"* also known as *"Emily: Maid of Morgan Point."* This handwritten copy was penned c.1836, not long after the battle of San Jacinto, and is now in the \archives of the University of Texas at Austin. A version close to this one was a favorite with Confederate soldiers, especially the Texans. The song has been changed and added to over the years.

**Martha Washington** was the first woman on U.S. currency; her face is on the 1886 $1 silver certificate bill. She also appears on the 1896 "Educational Series" $1 silver certificate, along with husband George.

"Where gold goes, blood flows!"

—Mrs. Ova Noss, one of the claimants to Victorio Peak, New Mexico

*Treasure: Lost, Found & Undiscovered*

"I concluded to make some pies and see if I could sell them to the miners for their lunches, as there were about one hundred men on the creek, doing their own cooking - there were plenty of dried apples and dried pealed peaches from Chili, pressed in the shape of a cheese, to be had, so I bought fat salt pork and made lard, and my venture was a success. I sold fruit pies for one dollar and a quarter a piece, and mince pies for one dollar and fifty cents. I sometimes made and sold, a hundred in a day, and not even a stove to bake them in, but had two small dutch ovens."......

—Mary Jane Caples

*Goldrush.com*

"I should like to tell you how the western people talk, if I had room. Their language is so singular that I could scarcely understand them, yet it was very amusing. In speaking of quantity, they say "heap of man, heap of water, she is heap sick", etc. If you ask, "How does your wife today?" "O, she is smartly better, I reckon, but she is powerful weak; she has been mighty bad. What's the matter with your eye?"

—Narcissa Whitman (in an 1836 letter to her sister Jane)

*Baby Doe Tabor, in her salad days.*

"A little further on, you stop before a small brass machine...Ha! Ha! It is a tailor. Yes, a veritable stitcher. Present a piece of cloth to it; it suddenly becomes agitated, it twists about, screams audibly...a needle sets to work; and lo and behold, the process of sewing goes on with feverish activity..."

—Giornale di Roma, reviewing an early sewing machine shown at the 1851 Crystal Palace exhibition in Hyde Park, London, England

The widow Cashman arrived on the streets of Boston, fresh from the potato famines in Ireland and with her daughters Ellen and Frances in tow. Sometime before 1869, the threesome paid for their way via Panama, and arrived in San Francisco, where Frances married an Irishman who had also spent time in Boston. But "Nellie" had different plans, and they involved the mining camps. Little is known about her time in San Francisco – but sometime in the early 1870s, Nellie and her mother left for Virginia City, NV, where Nellie opened a boardinghouse. It was a pattern Nellie was to continue for the next four decades.

By 1872, Nellie and Mrs. Cashman were in Pinoche, NV, a raw mining camp with two breweries, 72 saloons... and silver production that peaked at $5,500,000 that year. Nellie, though a woman of firm morals, and deeply Catholic, loved the excitement of the camp. She also enjoyed the company of men – and they enjoyed her. Nellie's biographer, Sally Zanjani, said,

"The members of the mining crowd showed themselves egalitarian enough to accept a woman so spirited and daring that she would go where they went and do as they did – especially if she agreed to open a boardinghouse."

Over the next decades, Nellie opened a series of hotels, restaurants and boardinghouses in various mining camps throughout California and Nevada; "There are no cockroaches in my kitchen and the flour is clean," she said of one. She fed and took care of the miners, even when they were sick or without money. Her boarding houses also frequently raised funds for various Catholic causes.

1845-1925

ANGEL OF THE KLONDIKE

ELLEN CASHMAN

# NELLIE CASHMAN

*Nellie Cashman*

In 1873, Nellie left Pinoche for the Cassiar district, the only woman in a company of 200-plus prospectors bound for the Klondike. She cheerfully endured the thousand-mile trip through snow and forest. "I have mushed with men, slept out in the open, traveled with them, and been with them constantly, and I have never been offered an insult. A woman is as safe among the miners as at her own fireside," Nellie later said. Once there, Nellie opened a combination saloon and boardinghouse.

She had closed the place for the winter and gone to Victoria until spring, when she heard her old friends in the Cassiar district were desperate. Their supplies were gone and scurvy had hit hard, but rescue groups had been driven back three times. Nellie, along with six hired men, set out with more than 1,500 pounds of potatoes, lime juice and other supplies. The trip took 77 days through storms and deep snow, but they arrived in time to save most of the men's lives. And Nellie acquired her best-known title, "Angel of the Klondike."

For the rest of her life, she traveled back and forth between mining towns, ranging from Tombstone, AZ down to Baja California up through the Chilkoot Pass and on to Fairbanks and Dawson, AK. She opened restaurants and hotels, many of them successful, along the way. On her last trip out of the Arctic, as an elderly woman, she mushed 1,500 miles in 17 days. She caught cold – something she laughingly noted happened every time she left Alaska – but this time, it turned into double pneumonia. She told the nuns at the Victoria hospital –the same institution she had helped fund with the miners' contributions of gold dust decades earlier – "I have come home to die." The Angel was no more.

Scurvy was the feared enemy of the mining camp – in just a few months, it transformed a strong, ruddy miner into an invalid with black-tinged skin. Old scars had reopened, and his teeth were loose in his jaws. Death soon followed. The only remedy was Vitamin C, gained from citrus juice, potatoes, ascorbic acid, or the old California Gold Rush remedy, pine needle tea.

# GOLD RUSH ERA CLOTHING

Although space limitations don't allow exhaustive detail, it's important to understand the basic person's everyday costume during the 1840s, and the decades soon after. Little was wasted; people's worn-out clothing, as well as leftover scraps, made their way into the period's quilts. And those clothing fibers and styles started trends of their own.

Before they made their pile, Californians needed their clothing to wear...and wear...and wear. Most clothing was made at home by the women of the family, or by a tailor or dressmaker. Although the sewing machine was in use by this period (more in Europe than America), most clothing was stitched by hand. By the full Gold Rush, enterprising merchants were offering the "California outfit:" a suit of clothing from head to toe, including hat and boots.

By the time men and women reached the goldfields, their clothing was well-worn; accounts mention stained shirts and long hemlines little more than rags. Dry goods and clothing were available from traveling peddlers, or could be purchased from "slop shops," small stores that were often nothing more than a tent. These items were high-priced, so much that miners would only reserve a good shirt for Sundays, and make do the rest of the week.

## For Men

Two styles of shirts were common: the curved shoulder version we know best (but quite new for the 1840s), as well as a bibbed or placketed front that could be unbuttoned and pushed back. Shirts were made of a wide variety of fabrics, including the small prints we know today as 'shirtings.' Dress shirts (white ones were "boiled," literally) had a thin collar, for attaching another collar, or a wide flat collar meant to fold over a cravat.

Men of all levels wore vests and waistcoats, of silks, wools and leather. The vest could be basic, or elaborately embroidered. Coats were thigh length, or in the case of

## For Women

The wrapper, a long loose robe made from light woolens (like challis) or linsey woolsey, could be worn corseted or not, and was comfortable for heavy work. (It also concealed a developing pregnancy.) Sometimes the neck was cut square, and fabrics pleated up to it to add more ease. Collars and cuffs could be added. (This outfit is also called a Mother Hubbard.) Sleeves were cut tight in "coat sleeve" style, or widened out in a bell sleeve. These were also made in cottons as the century progressed and cotton prices went down.

Ballgowns were worn for special occasions – assuming, of course, that the wearer could afford the many yards of fine silk needed, as well as fancy trims. (Velvet, though used to trim gowns, was considered a "day" fabric and rarely used.) Hooped skirts and petticoats held the skirt out, though not as far as later in the century.

Bodices were cut low, either square or in a V or curve; sleeves were tight or puffed, and kept short. Piping, lace, ribbons and rosettes were favorite trims; lace and ruffles could be added along the neckline for a wide collar look called a bertha. Cotton gowns were considered more informal, but many accounts mention them during dances in gold camps.

tailcoats, even longer, and made of checks, plaids and solids. These were worn with a 2-3"-wide strip of fabric tied in a small bow for a cravat – or a bandanna of silk or cotton.

Pants were heavy wool; for work, they were often made of heavy canvas or cotton duck. ("Levis," the heavy denim pants, arrived in the goldfields in the 1850s.) Suspenders helped keep everything up. Buttoned details and deep pockets came in handy.

Jewelry was simple. Photographs from this period often show individuals of both sexes wearing gold nugget chains, necklaces, etc.

### And Outside: For outer clothing, women wore mantuas, mantillas and other styles of short capes, topped with 60" or wider woolen paisley shawls. (These shawls were often the equivalent of an engagement notice, and the prized possession of many a married woman.) Women's low bonnets helped keep rain and snow off; they could have been lined with ruffles, but had a curtain, or brevelot, hanging down the back to hide the neck. (Showing the neck was thought indecent!) Long hooded cloaks were called "old women cloaks" and generally avoided. Men are mentioned as wearing cloaks and suits of rubber, as well as heavy boots; women have been documented borrowing men's boots, so they may have worn rubber outfits, too.

# PRAIRIE STAR

Stars dance across a creamy prairie in this old-as-the-hills quilt design. Stars were used by early emigrants for navigation, but they were also no doubt a comfort on a sparkling moonlit night. The Eight-Pointed Star is one of quilting's oldest patterns, but has been a design staple in everything from dishware to furniture to...barns! (Star patterns were thought to convey special powers by some groups, like the Pennsylvania Dutch, and along with hex signs, were painted on barns for protection.) We know this pinwheel-type star best today as LeMoyne Star, most probably named for Jean-Baptiste LeMoyne de Bienville and his brother Pierre, the founders of New Orleans. The smaller miniature size was a special favorite of 19th century quiltmakers; it used up scraps more effectively, and could easily be combined with all-purpose muslin. Give your background a more heavenly tint with a metallic cream print...or use a white-on-white monoprint for textured results. Stick to one fabric for a seamless overall look.

Note: This quilt has been adapted from the original to better fit a modern-sized bed.

## HOW TO MAKE PRAIRIE STAR

**FINISHED QUILT SIZE: 84" X 90" (14 ROWS OF 15 - 6" FINISHED BLOCKS)**

### FABRIC REQUIREMENTS

Assorted light, medium and dark fabric scraps (blocks): 5 1/4 yards

(California Gold scraps could be part of the mix)

Background fabric (muslin used in original quilt): 6 1/2 yards

Backing: 7 1/2 yards (cut 3 panels 31" x 88" and join vertically)

Batting: 89" x 94"

Binding: 2/3 yard

This version of LeMoyne uses 2 alternating fabrics for each star: 4 California Gold A patches and 4 brown print A reverse patches. The star block is filled in with corners and outer triangles of a third fabric – cream muslin.

### CUTTING REQUIREMENTS

#### Blocks

**Plain Alternating Blocks** (105 - 6" finished squares needed)

Cut 6 1/2" squares from background fabric, for a total of 105 squares. These will be alternated with the LeMoyne Star blocks shown on the following page.

#### LeMoyne (Eight-Pointed) Stars –

105 pieced 6" finished blocks

Use the actual-size block diagram to trace an A and Ar star diamond pattern, B triangle and C square patterns; add 1/4" seams.

**Tip:** C patches are also 2" squares! Cut them directly from the fabric, instead of making a template.

You need to cut cut 4 A patches, plus 4 Ar (or reverse – turn your pattern wrong side up), for each block. Use your fabric scraps to cut 420 A and 420 Ar patches for the entire quilt; you may want to reserve each fabric for just 1 star – or mix and match by shade to give a more blended effect. If you wish to copy the quilt shown, each block uses 4 A patches of 1 fabric, and 4 Ar patches of a second, slightly contrasting, fabric.

From the remaining background fabric, cut 4 B and 4 C patches for each block (total of 420 each for the entire quilt).

## Backing, Batting and Binding

See General Instructions on pages 36-38.

## Block Assembly

### LEMOYNE STAR BLOCKS (6" FINISHED):

1   Lay out all the patches for one block, so you can see them as you sew.

2.  Take a second block's worth of patches. Match 1 A diamond with its alternating Ar (reverse) diamond and stitch together along 1 of the 2 longest sides. Repeat until you have four pairs of joined A/Ar diamonds. Press. (Note: stitching the final block will be easier if you begin and end 1/4" from the patch edge; take time to mark and sew one block's worth of diamonds this way, and you'll see what we mean. Both machine and hand stitchers will find this especially useful.)

**Block Diagram**

3. Arrange the A/Ar diamond pairs in a circle. For each pair, fit a corner square in the pieced middle – match and pin one edge of the C patch in place, then sew from outside in, stopping and starting 1/4" from the edge. Stop your machine, leaving the needle still in the 'down' position, 1/4" from the edge.

4. Without taking your block from under the needle, or out of the machine, lift up the C's other edge and fit it to the other side of the diamond pair; pin if needed. Stitch, stopping 1/4" from the outer edge. Press your set-in corner seam flat.

**Tip:** Try piecing these blocks by hand! You'll find the pivoting and seams easier, and they go together amazingly fast, once you've done one block and worked the kinks out of the technique. Either way, you'll find that the first block takes a while, but succeeding blocks get easier and easier. California wasn't reached in a day, after all...

5. Join 2 pairs of paired diamond/corner squares, stopping and starting 1/4" from the joined patch edges.

6. Fit in a B long triangle patch into the centers of each diamond foursome, using the same method as for the corner squares. (Note: some stitchers prefer waiting to do this until after Step 7, then adding all 4 B patches to the block, one by one. Try it both ways, and see what you think.)

7. Stitch both foursomes together. If you haven't already done so, add the rest (or all) of the B patches. Carefully press your block to finish. (See General Instructions, page 34.)

8. Your first block is done! Use the same process to stitch 104 more blocks, for a total of 105. Press each block as you finish it.

# Quilt Assembly

## STITCHING THE TOP

1. Put the pieced star blocks in one pile, and the plain blocks in another. Deal them out card-fashion in 14 rows of 15 blocks, for an overall random look, beginning with a plain block on the first row, then alternating stars and plain blocks. (Use the quilt diagram for help.) Resist your urge to 'match!'

2. Take at least 6 steps back, then check the overall design. Too many golds in one corner? Blacks got all bunched up in the center? Now is the time to carefully move star blocks around for a more blended look. Remember: 'ugly' blocks actually help competing fabrics blend together better. (Think strangers at a cocktail party.) Walk away, if possible, for at least an hour before you begin stitching. Take another look, and adjust wherever is needed.

3. Take up the blocks – first row only – with the top left (plain) block first on the pile. Alternately stitch plain and star blocks together, then join those pairs for Row 1. (Remember: the more consistent your seamlines are, the better these blocks will fit together.) Take special pains to keep your star points crisp, if at all possible.

4. Press Row 1, then lay it back into place. Go through the same process for Rows 2-14, stitching as evenly as you can. Press all rows one more time, then join, using the outside block seams as a stitching guide. (Double-check to make sure your blocks are alternating, row by row, as shown in the assembly diagram.) Press your finished quilt top.

**Tip:** Want to make your quilt top even more accurate? Wait to cut the alternating block patches until all of your star blocks are pieced. (You'll still need to cut B and C patches right away.) Measure all of your star blocks after piecing, then use the most common size as your "golden mean." (Trim the other blocks slightly to fit together better; or plan to 'fudge' to keep the points as crisp as possible when joining blocks.) Use the golden mean size for measuring and cutting your plain alternating blocks.

**Assembly Diagram**

# Finishing the Top

Layer your top with batting and backing; baste. Tie or quilt as you like (see General Instructions on page 38); this style looks especially 'twinkly' when quilted in an allover pattern, like diagonally-spaced lines. After quilting or tying, bind to finish.

STATE OF THE UNION, *c.1885, collection of Jeananne Wright.*

# STATE OF THE UNION

This sawtooth beauty inspired the scrappy Girls of the Golden West quilt, as well as the pieced outer border on the Girls' redwork version. It takes a page from the traditional pieced Union block and expands it with another edging of pieced triangles, Square within A Square style. The California Gold alternating blocks and triangles help stretch the original quilt into a double bed size. In this case, the block's been increased three inches larger to 13", so the quilt will fit a queen bed, instead. The setting and overall look, however, remain the same.

Don't let the many small pieced triangle squares discourage you – this is a pattern rarely done. While piecing the first block, you'll be teaching yourself how to sew and fit triangles evenly. By the second block, your skills are already learned, and you'll find the blocks coming together much more smoothly. (Trust this quilter – she knows from experience.)

At least three decades' worth of fabrics were used in the original c. 1880 quilt. This is an excellent opportunity to clear out your multi-decade scrap bag, as well. Any leftover triangles can go into the Girls – or vice versa. Or save them for a miniature version of Centennial Triangles.

## HOW TO MAKE STATE OF THE UNION

(ADAPTED FROM THE ORIGINAL QUILT)

FINISHED QUILT SIZE: 86" X 104"

(4 ROWS OF 5 - 13" BLOCKS, ON POINT)

### FABRIC REQUIREMENTS

Green (blocks): 1 yard

Cream (blocks): 5 yards

Assorted light (not too light), medium and dark fabric scraps (blocks and outer border): approximately 4 yards

California Gold (alternating blocks, triangles and outer border): 4 1/2 yards

Backing: 7 1/2 yards (join 3 panels of 36 1/2" x 90" for a 90" x 108" backing)

Batting: 90" x 108" rectangle

Binding: 1 yard

**Tip:** Watch your lights! To keep the contrast strong between the sawtoothed triangle squares and the cream background, use only a few light-colored fabrics. The traditional choice for the cream was muslin, either from yardage or a sugar or flour sack. You can give this piece even more interest by substituting a cream-on-cream monoprint.

## CUTTING REQUIREMENTS

### Blocks

#### Pieced State of the Union blocks –

13" finished blocks (20 needed)

Note: Be sure to read through the entire instructions before you begin to cut! Use the Girls of the Golden West scrappy quilt for block and top instructions (pages 41-44), and the Girls of the Golden West redwork quilt (pages 49, 54) for the outer pieced border. Instead of the women, though, substitute a central green square for each pieced block.

*From green:* Cut 20 - 6 1/2" squares

*From cream and assorted scraps:*

1. Cut enough for 20 blocks, using the instructions for the Golden West scrappy quilt. (You may choose to cut your triangles, like Triangle Rule #1 on page 45, or quick-piece them with the method described on pages 33 and 53. Either way, you need 72 x 20 = 1440 pieced 1 1/2" triangle squares. Trim to size, if needed.) Also be sure to cut inner block setting triangles from cream, as well.

2. You'll also need cream and assorted scraps for the 2" pieced quilt border: Use the instructions for the pieced border on the Golden West redwork version – you need 37 - 2 1/2" pieced triangle squares each (one

muslin, one scrap) for the top and bottom of the quilt, and 48 - 2 1/2" triangle squares each for the sides, for a total of 266 2 1/2" triangle squares. Trim to size, if needed.)

3. For the inner block borders, cut 2" strips from the width of the remaining yardage; you need 36 strips. Cut these in turn into 2" squares; 36 are needed for each block. Cut those in half diagonally to make 72 triangles per block x 20 blocks = a total of 1440 triangles needed.

*From light and dark fabric scraps:* Cut exactly the same amounts as given in Steps 2 and 3 of cream, for both the outer quilt border and the inner block borders.

**From California Gold:**
*For the blocks:* Cut 4 - 1 1/2" squares for each block, to be used in the second inner block border. Four squares x 20 blocks = a total of 80 squares needed. *(Wait to cut these squares until you've done the larger patches below first!)* **Note:** The block diagram for this quilt – as well as the Girls of the Golden West quilt – uses these California Gold squares...but the original State of the Union quilt does not. If you'd prefer, cut, sew and substitute 80 more 1" finished pieced triangle squares in their place.

**Alternating Blocks, Side Large Triangles and Corner Triangles** (varying sizes)
Outer (4" finished) Border

**From California Gold:**
*Cut the outer border strips first:*
Two 4 1/2" x 78 1/2" top/bottom strips
Two 4 1/2" x 104 1/2" side strips

Use the instructions in the *Girls of the Golden West* pattern to size and cut the rest of the patches. You need 12 alternating blocks, 14 long outer triangles and 4 corner triangles. (Once you're done, then finish by cutting the 1 1/2" squares mentioned above.) **Note:** The "Floating" factor, mentioned on page 42, will also work for this quilt, if you're feeling uncertain about exactly matching all pieced seams. If so, then leave the length meant for your outer borders uncut for now. *(See Quilt Assembly on page 90.)*

**Tip:** If at all possible, cut your largest patches first from the yardage. Then cut the rest of the patches, from the largest on down. This way, you won't run out of fabric as easily, or have to piece smaller fabric scraps together to get the larger patches.

## Backing, Batting and Binding
See General Instructions on pages 36-38.

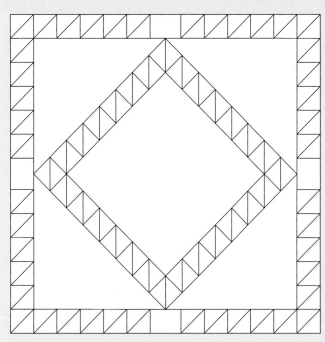

**Block Diagram, finished size 13"**
*Note: see page 53 for a handy Quick-Pieced Triangle Square method.*

# Block Assembly

Use the instructions in Girls of the Golden West on page 40 to piece your basic block – but substitute the green 6 1/2" square for the central Lady square. Refer to the block diagram and the quilt photo. Remember: the muslin points face away from the center in the first border (surrounding the square), and toward the center in the second, outer border. Think 'positive'(cream)/'negative' (scraps) if that helps. Stitch one block first; this will be your slowest one, by far. (The others will go much more quickly!) Lay the first block aside for reference as you stitch 19 more, for a total of 20 blocks.

**Tip:** Note the pieced border corners – they generally set the pattern for the row, or announce what's coming next. But don't let yourself get too caught up in making all the pieced block borders exactly alike – the blocks in State of the Union are not all pieced exactly the same way. The important thing is not to sew 2 cream triangles next to each other – or 2 scrap triangles next to each other.

**Tip:** Looking for an easier way to stitch across all those points? When you're pressing the pieced triangle square strips, press the seams between the squares away from the triangles. The seamlines form an X – stitch right through the center of each for crisp points. For best results, check every single pieced triangle square, and trim to size so they're all 1 1/2" square. (Patience, in this case, pays off.)

## Quilt Border Assembly (2")

Remember those 3" squares of muslin and vari-colored scraps you cut earlier? Match a muslin triangle and a print triangle, stitch for a pieced triangle square. Join 43 randomly, all facing the same direction, for the top and bottom borders, and 53 each for the side borders, for a total of 192.

# Quilt Assembly

## STITCHING THE TOP

1. Lay out the pieced blocks, alternating blocks, larger outer triangles and corner triangles, using the quilt diagram and the quilt photo for help.

2. Join the different elements of each row, and press. Join the rows together.

## Adding Borders

1. Press your top, then measure it carefully, top/bottom and sides. Trim slightly to 74 1/2" x 92 1/2". (The "floating" factor helps you match a pieced top and its pieced borders more evenly.)

2. Add the pieced border strips to the top and bottom of the quilt first, then match and add the side strips. (Note: the muslin triangles in each border face away from the pieced blocks. See the quilt photo for help.) If you've waited to cut the outer plain border, now's the time to measure your quilt again – preferably through the center. Use those measurements to cut your border strips. Or – add the border strips you've already cut: top/bottom, then sides. Press all to finish.

# Finishing the Quilt

Layer with batting and backing; baste. Tie or quilt as you like (see General Instructions on page 38); the original quilt shown was marked with vertical lines about 1" apart, then quilted in an allover pattern. Bind to finish the quilt.

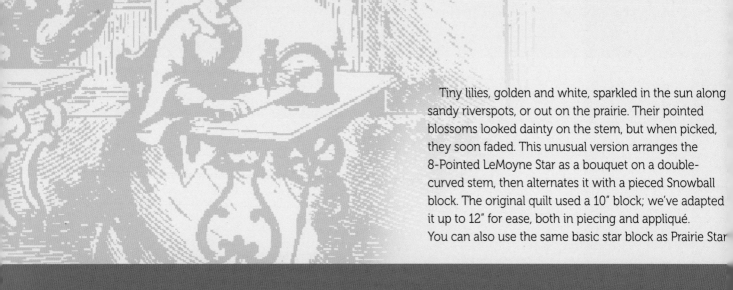

Tiny lilies, golden and white, sparkled in the sun along sandy riverspots, or out on the prairie. Their pointed blossoms looked dainty on the stem, but when picked, they soon faded. This unusual version arranges the 8-Pointed LeMoyne Star as a bouquet on a double-curved stem, then alternates it with a pieced Snowball block. The original quilt used a 10" block; we've adapted it up to 12" for ease, both in piecing and appliqué. You can also use the same basic star block as Prairie Star

# SAND LILIES

## HOW TO MAKE SAND LILIES

(NORTH CAROLINA LILY VARIATION)
FINISHED QUILT SIZE: 90" X 108"

**Note:** This quilt combines piecing and appliqué in an unusual way, and uses the LeMoyne Star block in Prairie Star as a unit in the much larger Lily block here. Read the pattern through carefully before you begin to cut and stitch, so you understand how the various elements of each block fit together.

**Tip:** Prefer a shorter quilt? Omit 1 row of blocks on the shorter side, and you'll have a 90" x 96" quilt – still perfectly adequate for a queen-sized bed. The blocks will be arranged in an 8 x 7 set, for a total of 56 blocks – 28 of each type. (See below for specifics.) Use the 9 leftover blocks for pillows or a matching wallhanging.

## FABRIC REQUIREMENTS

California Gold (blocks): 2 1/2 yards

Brown print (blocks): 2 1/2 yards

Green solid (blocks – both Lily and Snowball blocks, outer pieced border): 5 yards

Cream muslin (blocks and outer pieced border): 8 yards

Backing: 8 1/3 yards (cut 3 - 38" x 94" lengths, and join vertically for backing)

Batting: 94" x 112" square

Binding: 1 yard

## CUTTING REQUIREMENTS

**Blocks**: (12" finished – 31 Lily blocks and 32 Snowball blocks, arranged in a 7 x 9 block set, for 63 blocks total)

*From white:* Cut 32 -12 1/2" squares for the Snowball blocks. Also cut 31 - 6 1/2" squares for the Lily blocks, as well as the triangles for the pieced Sawtooth outer border. (See Border cutting instructions on page 35.) Use the rest of the white for piecing the LeMoyne Star units. You need 4 B triangles and 4 C squares for each LeMoyne Star unit; 12 of each are needed for a Lily block x 31 blocks = 372 B and 372 C patches.

**SAND LILIES,** *c.1885, collection of Cathy Litwinow.*

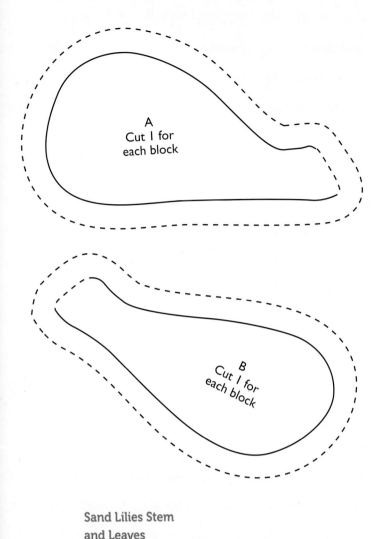

A
Cut 1 for
each block

B
Cut 1 for
each block

Sand Lilies Stem
and Leaves
(actual size for 12" blocks)

*From green:* Cut 4 - 6 1/2" squares for a Snowball block; 4 x 32 blocks = 128 squares total. Also cut triangles for the pieced Sawtooth outer borders. (See Border cutting instructions on page 99.)

*Stems:* cut enough folded stem strips to make the straight and the curved sections (plus a little extra for seam allowances).

Make a pattern for the A and B leaves. Trace each pattern on the fabric, then cut outside the traced line, leaving about 1/4" for a turn-under allowance. (See the Turkey Tracks pattern on page 116 for cutting, basting and appliqué help, as well as General Instructions on page 34.) You need 32 each of A and B leaves, for a total of 64. Use the rest of the green to make bias "stems" for appliqué; see the box for help.

*From California Gold:* Cut 4 Ar diamonds for each LeMoyne Star unit; you need 12 Ar pieces for each Lily block x 31 blocks = 372 Ar pieces total.

*From brown print:* Cut 4 A diamonds for each LeMoyne Star unit; you need 12 A diamonds for each Lily block x 31 blocks = 372 A total.

## Borders: (3" finished pieced Sawtooth triangle rows – 2 sides only)

*From white:* Cut a 10" square diagonally twice for 4 triangles; you need 8 squares, for a total of 32 triangles. (See "Triangle Rules" on page 45 for cutting help.)

*From green:* Cut the same as white.

## Bias Stems for Appliqué

Green stems for appliquéd flowers add a realistic touch. Commercially-folded binding can be substituted for stems; look for thinner versions about 1/4" for better results. The problem, though, is matching the shade – and in that case, it's easier to make these strips yourself. You can follow this same method by cutting straight-grain strips, and using them for straight-line appliqué. A bias approach, though, gives just enough ease to accomplish your curved lines gracefully. Here we go:

1. Cut as large a square as possible. Fold it in half diagonally.

2. Trim off the folded edge evenly, giving you 2 large triangles. *(Leave them matched to each other!)* Using your ruler, continue to cut 3/4"-wide strips, following the cut edges.

3. Join the strips together diagonally for 1 *long* piece of bias binding strip. Using spray starch and/or a water bottle for help, press each of the sides in toward the center, giving you a 1/4" tri-folded binding strip.

4. Continue to do this until you have enough for all of the Lily blocks...or make enough for the first 6 blocks, then cut and press more binding strips as needed. You need 22" - 25" for each Lily block.

**Tip:** The original quilt only had pieced border rows on 2 sides. It's not difficult to add this border on the other 2 sides, as well. Increase both green and cream yardage another 1/2 yard each, then cut the same amount of triangles, plus 4 - 3 1/2" corner blocks. (You'll have leftovers.) Piece and fit the border strips as given in the stitching directions, but use 11 each of green and white triangles, with the white corner squares added on each end of the new side border strips.

## Backing, Batting and Binding

See General Instructions on pages 36-38.

**Sand Lilies Block - in progress**

# Block Assembly

### LILY BASIC BLOCK: (12" FINISHED)

1. Begin with the LeMoyne Star block on (see pages 80 and 96). Like the Prairie Star quilt where it is featured, this version of LeMoyne uses 2 alternating fabrics for each star. In this quilt, its 4 California Gold A patches and 4 brown print patches, filled in with corners and outer triangles of a third fabric – cream muslin.

2. Follow the Prairie Star general instructions to stitch a LeMoyne Star block (referred to from now on as a *unit*). Press the block carefully and use it as a reference, along with the block diagram.

3. You need 3 LeMoyne Star units for every Lily block. Since there are 31 Lily blocks, you need to piece 93 LeMoyne Star units total, all made with the same gold/brown color combination.

4. Take the white 6 1/2" squares. Combine 1 with 3 LeMoyne Star units to make a basic Lily block (without appliqué).

5. Refer to the finished Lily block diagram, to help you visualize the following steps.

**Sand Lilies Block - finished**

## Ready?

6. Pick open a few stitches from each LeMoyne star edge where it will eventually be touching an appliquéd stem.

7. Appliqué stems and A/B leaves in place, using the block diagram, appliqué suggestions in the Turkey Tracks pattern and General Instructions for help. Tip: Don't pull the curved stem section too tight as you stitch – this will cause the block to pucker or bow. Instead, lightly pin the stem in place and remove pins as you stitch. Gently guiding the curve with a toothpick is also helpful.

8. Slide the stem ends gently underneath the loosened LeMoyne Star points, then appliqué all back in place.

9. Hooray – your first Lily block is done! You were learning technique with this one; the next blocks will stitch much more easily. Make 30 more blocks, for a total of 31.

**Tip:** Although fine cotton thread has been used in appliqué for centuries, try a fine silk thread instead. It lets you do better, stronger stitching, and the thread visually "disappears" into the fabric it's stitched on! Four colors will cover nearly all your stitching needs: cream, tan, gray and black. The only drawback: because of its tendency to fray, you can generally only use a 12" length of thread. Look for a Japanese-made thread, and a higher thread number: #100 is good, #200 is even better.

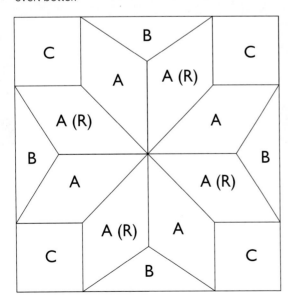

LeMoyne Star block

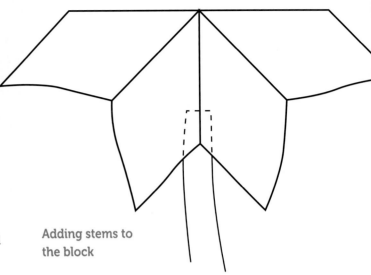

Adding stems to the block

## Snowball Basic Block: (12" finished)

1. The Snowball is the sturdy workhouse block that lets its fancy sister, the Lily, shine. Take a look at the finished block. You're going to use an easy stitch-trim-and-flip method that uses overlapping squares to make this block.

Snowball Block

2. Lay out a 12 1/2" white square and 4 green 6 1/2" squares; set aside 3 of the green squares for later. Match the remaining square in the top left corner of the larger white square, then stitch diagonally. (For best results, mark the sewing line diagonally before you stitch; see A right.)

3. Trim to 1/4" on the outer side of the stitched seam, and discard the trimmings (B).

4. Press back the stitched corner smoothly.

(Try ironing from the back first, pressing the seam-line toward the green triangle.) Continue until all 4 corners on the block are done (see C and D).

5. First block...wasn't that easy? You need 31 more Snowball blocks, for a total of 32 blocks.

**Piecing a Snowball Block**

A: Fit your 6" square in 1 corner, then stitch diagonally.

B: Trim 1/4" away from the stitched line.

C and D: Fold back the new corner triangle, press.

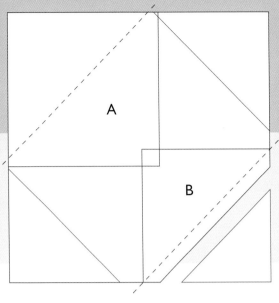

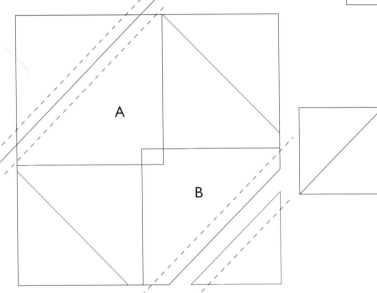

A. Mark your corner diagonal line, then sew 1/4" away – twice.

B. B. Trim on the marked line and you have a bonus pieced triangle square for another project!

**Tip:** Hate wasting fabric? Try this frugal alternative; you'll end up with a stitched Snowball block *plus* 4 small pieced triangle squares! (Yes, they can be trimmed down and used in the State of the Union or Girls of the Golden West quilts, too. Or add them to a Centennial Triangles design you've been pondering.)

**Tip:** The Snowball is an amazingly versatile design! Try experimenting with a 6" finished Snowball block, alternating with a 6" Nine Patch block (from Golden Years) or a single 6" LeMoyne Star unit *(or both!)* for a completely new look. You need a 6 1/2" white square, plus 4 - 3 1/2" squares of contrasting fabric. (For continuity, use the same fabric for all 4 squares.) Follow the stitching process described above.

# Quilt Assembly

## STITCHING THE TOP

1. Using the Assembly Diagram for help, alternate 4 Lily and 5 Snowball blocks in a 9-block row, beginning and ending with a Snowball block.

2. For the second 9-block row, alternate 5 Lily and 4 Snowball blocks, beginning and ending with a Lily block.

3. Repeat these rows until you've laid out 7 rows of 9 blocks.

4. Take another look at the Assembly Diagram. Notice how the Lily blocks are positioned so they generally point away from the sides of the quilt, and toward its center? Reposition the Lily blocks as needed to follow the overall pattern.

Assembly Diagram

5. Stitch the blocks in each row together; press carefully and lay the stitched row back in place. Repeat until all the rows are stitched, double-checking Lily block placements occasionally with the Assembly Diagram.

6. Give the stitched rows a final press, then join the rows together.

# Adding Borders

1. Arrange and join green and white border triangles together, alternating colors as shown in the quilt photo. Use the border triangle count on the Quilt Assembly Diagram as your guide; each border strip takes 15 each of green and white border triangles, for a total of 30 green and 30 white triangles. Press each border strip carefully after stitching.

2. Notice that in both the quilt photo and the diagram, the triangles in the borders do not match the blocks evenly – and the border strip is too long! No worries – this contributes to the folk art look of the original design. Center the border strip on each of the long sides of the quilt; stitch, then trim the border to fit. Press carefully.

# Finishing the Quilt

Layer with batting and backing; baste. Tie or quilt as you like. (See General Instructions on pages 36-38. The plain central space in the center of each Snowball is tailor-made for a quilting motif, like Wild Rose on page 44.) Bind to finish the quilt.

**Buffalo Bill" William Cody:** *scout, buffalo hunter...and (largely unsuccessful) miner. He is remembered best today for his lavish Wild West shows.*

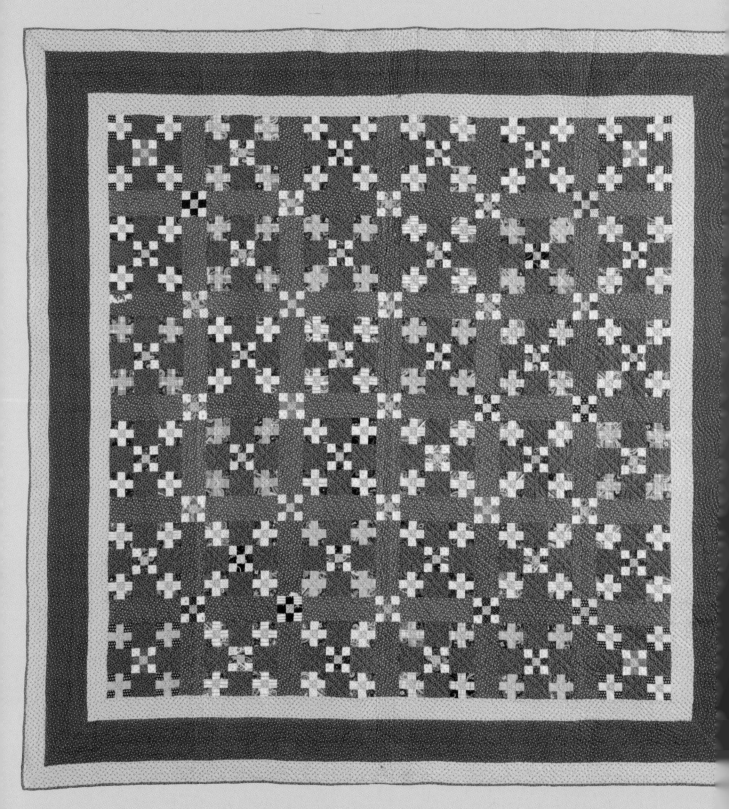

FRAMED NINE PATCH, *c.1885, collection of Jeananne Wright.*

# FRAMED NINE-PATCH

The Nine Patch is one of the oldest quilt designs. It dates back literally thousands of years, and is found in everything from floors to dishware to quilts. Pioneer quiltmakers loved this pattern because it wasted very little of their precious fabric and was easy to stitch, both by hand and machine. While they usually cut and hand-pieced squares; this version recommends machine strip piecing. You'll get done in a fraction of the time!

California Gold sparkles in the centers of the mini-Nine Patches repeated throughout this c.1885 version, both by themselves in the sashing intersections, and again in the larger-set Nine Patch blocks. Old-time quilters might have waited to purchase the sashing and border fabrics until they finished the blocks needed.

## HOW TO MAKE A FRAMED NINE PATCH

**FINISHED QUILT SIZE: 85" X 85"**

### FABRIC REQUIREMENTS

Assorted light and dark fabric scraps (blocks): 3 1/2 yards

California Gold (blocks): 1/3 yard

Double pink (blocks): 1 1/2 yards

Green (sashing): 1 5/8 yards

Yellow (inner and outer borders): 2 5/8 yards

*(substitute 1 1/3 yards if you plan to piece the border strips)*

Green (middle border): 2 1/2 yards

*(substitute 1 1/4 yards if you plan to piece the border strips)*

Backing: 7 7/8 yards

Batting: 89" x 89" square

Binding: 5/8 yard

### CUTTING REQUIREMENTS

#### BLOCKS

Mini-Nine Patches – 205 - 3" blocks (25 for sashes, 180 for Framed Nine Patch blocks)

*From light and dark fabric scraps:* Cut 1 1/2" strips

*From California Gold:* Cut 1 1/2" strips

Framed Nine Patch Blocks (36 needed)

*From double pink:* Cut 144 - 3 1/2" squares (4 per block)

#### SASHING

*From green:* Cut 60 - 3 1/2" x 9 1/2" strips

**Tip:** Unless you are cutting longer border strips, use the width of the fabric to cut sashing and patches from your fabric yardage. Always cut the longest and largest patches first.

## Borders

*From yellow:*
Cut 4 - 2 1/2" x 75" inner border strips

Cut 4 - 2 1/2" x 87" outer border strips *(extra added to make mitering borders easier. Piece strips together if you chose the smaller yardage)*

*From green:* Cut 4 - 4 1/2" x 83" middle border strips

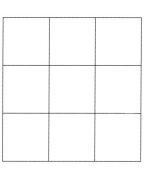

Basic Nine Patch Block (3" finished)

Framed Nine Patch Block (9" finished)

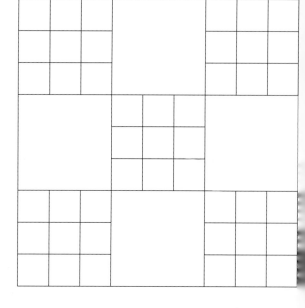

## Backing, Batting and Binding

See General Instructions on pages 36-38.

# Block Assembly

### MINI-NINE PATCHES (3" FINISHED)

1. You need at least 3 different strips for each block: 1 light, 1 dark and 1 CA (California) Gold. (Add more strips to copy the random look in the original quilt, and make multiple blocks at the same time.)

2. Sandwich 1 CA Gold between 2 darks; sew strips together.

3. Sandwich 1 dark between 2 lights; sew together.

4. Press, then cut 1 1/2" wedges from the sewn units.

5. You need 1 CA Gold wedge, and 2 dark/light wedges for each mini-block. Lay out wedges, using the block diagram, stitch, then join rows. Press as you go.

6. Use the same process with the rest of your fabrics to make 205 total mini-blocks.

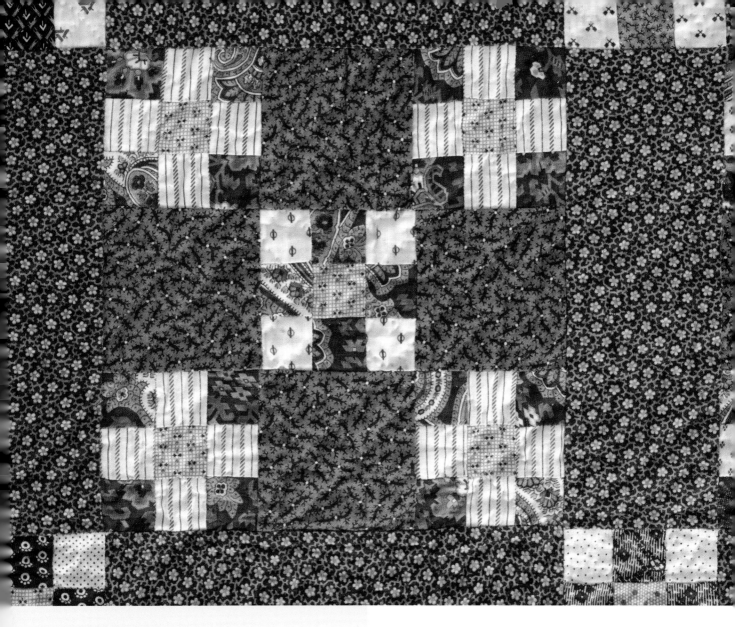

## Framed Nine Patches (9" finished)

1. You need 5 mini-blocks and 4 double pink patches for each block. Lay out rows, as shown in the block diagram, stitch. Join the rows.

2. Use the remaining mini-blocks and pink patches to make 36 blocks.

**Tip:** Pressing is important! Iron first from the back, using the point of your iron to push seam allowances flat (and preferably in the same direction). This helps prevent distortion when ironing on top of the block.

# Quilt Assembly

### STITCHING THE TOP

1. You need 36 Framed Nine Patch blocks, 25 mini-Nine Patches and the 60 green sashing strips. Lay these out in rows, using the Assembly Diagram as a guide. *(The blocks are in a 6 x 6 set – 6 rows by 6 rows, separated by sashing.)*

2. Stitch blocks and sashes together for a block row, then sashes and mini-Nine Patches together for a sash row. (Alternate these rows.) Stitch the rows together to finish your pieced quilt top. Press.

## Adding Borders

1. You will add all 3 of the borders to the quilt top at the same time. Sounds hard – but it's actually much easier to do it this way!

2. Find the center of all 3 strips; place a pin there for reference.

3. Match pins on an inner yellow and middle green border strip; stitch strips together lengthwise.

4. Match pins on the sewn double-strip and the outer yellow strip; stitch together lengthwise. (Your border ends will not be even – don't worry!)

5. Repeat for 3 more border strip units.

# Finishing the Top

1. Find the center on 1 side of your pieced Nine Patch top. Match it to the center of a border strip unit (yellow inner border toward the Nine Patch top) and pin. Smooth and pin the rest of the border strip in place.

2. Start 1/4" in from the top's edge, and stitch. Stop when you're 1/4" from the edge on the other side of the strip.

3. Add the other 3 border strip units, using the same method.

4. Miter corners by diagonally folding back the border unit until it matches the other border unit on that side. (See border diagram for help.) Press.

5. Use the ironed foldline as a stitching line to finish mitering the corners. (Alternate method: fold back diagonally, press, then hand-stitch each miter to finish.)

6. Trim away extra fabric. Repeat this process for the other 3 mitered corners. Press your finished quilt top.

**Tip:** Fold back the extra fabric on each sewn border strip unit and pin, before you add the next border strip unit. Do the top/bottom border strip units first, then sides.

7. Layer with batting and backing; baste. Tie or quilt as you like (see General Instructions on page 38), then bind to finish the quilt.

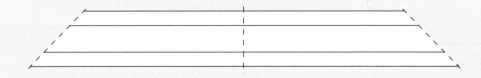

Center and sew the 3 border strips together for a combined border strip. Remember: this will be longer than the quilt top sides so you have extra for mitering the corners.

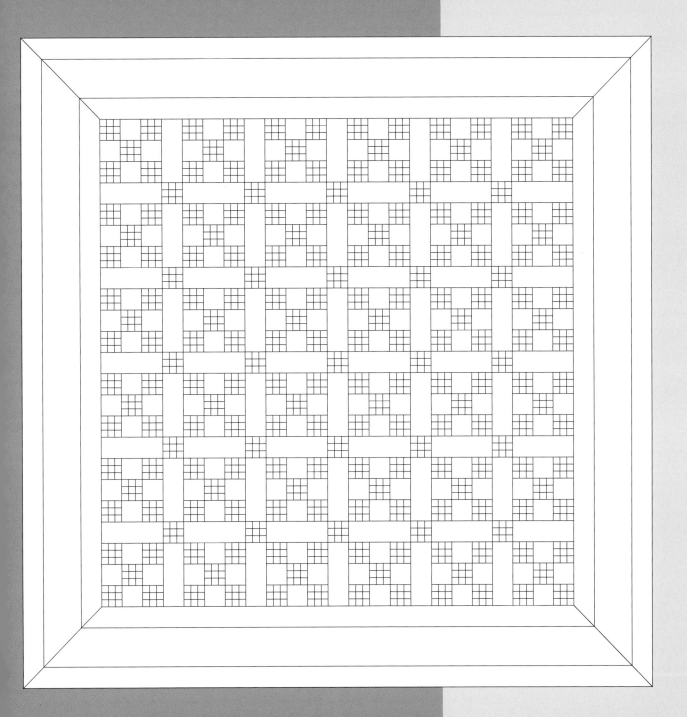

Assembly Diagram

Center and sew combined
border strips on, one at a time,
then miter the corners.

**GOLDEN YEARS,** *2009, made by Dawn Cumings and Cindy Brick. Picture this quilt in garden pastels or jewel tones – it will work with any color scheme, as long as the background fabric is dark enough for the pieced Nine Patch blocks to "disappear" into it.*

# GOLDEN YEARS

Nine Patch blocks twinkle in and out of sight on this wall/snuggle quilt, thanks to a sly trick with fabric – use the same print for background, sashing and parts of the 'disappearing' Nine Patch blocks! The California Gold-style intersection squares are the only element that holds steady throughout the quilt. Think of it as a chance to experiment with your favorite fabrics – as little as a fat eighth or fat quarter of several fabrics will do the trick in the Nine Patches. We also provide an early Thirties quilting motif that combines diamonds with simple cables. . Inspirations for this quilt: a Paul Pilgrim sampler that mixes modern fabrics and antique blocks in a "shadow" arrangement; Beth Gutcheon's "The Goose Is Loose"...and David Bowie's rowdy anthem to aging and fame, "Golden Years."

## HOW TO MAKE GOLDEN YEARS

(TIPPED NINE PATCH VARIATION)     FINISHED QUILT SIZE: 50" X 50"

Note: This quilt uses the same 'background' for sashing, as well as parts of the Nine Patch blocks, letting the blocks slowly (but only visually) "disappear" into the background while the golden intersection squares "float" on top. Take special care when choosing this background fabric; it should be something with an overall pattern or texture that will still read as 'continuous,' even when cut. Stay away from plaids, stripes and larger-scale prints; these are wonderful in the Nine Patch blocks, but will visually disrupt the overall effect if used as the 'background' fabric, instead.

You will need to take the same care when choosing an outer border fabric; it also has "disappearing" blocks that are better displayed with a more neutral fabric.

The quilt pictured uses a pebbly brown texture print, splashed lightly with metallics, as the background. A darker texture print in the same family of brown neutrals is used for a border fabric. Other possibilities include small-scale shirtings or florals (really small scale); monoprints; batiks, or even solids.

## FABRIC REQUIREMENTS

Assorted fabric scraps (blocks): 7/8 yard

Background fabric (tan in pictured quilt): 1 1/2 yard

Darker brown: 1/4 yard

Gold: 1/8 yard

Darker gold: 1/4 yard

Green (inner border) 1/3 yard

Darker brown (outer border): 1 1/2 yards

Backing: 3 1/8 yards (join 2 - 27 1/2" x 54" panels)

Batting: 54" x 54" square

Binding: 1/2 yard

## CUTTING REQUIREMENTS

This quilt uses 2 types of Nine Patch blocks – a traditional version, using a mixed 3 x 3 set of squares, and a "disappearing" version that eventually substitutes background fabric for all but a few squares. Both squares may be positioned four different directions for different effects – so don't hesitate to experiment until you get the look you want.

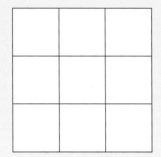

Basic Nine Patch Block
6" finished

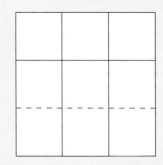

"Disappearing" Nine Patch Block
6" finished

# Blocks

Traditional Nine Patch Blocks (6" finished – 9 needed) (A)

From assorted fabric scraps: Cut a variety of 2 1/2"-wide strips, no longer than 20" each. You need some for the Disappearing Nine Patch blocks, as well.

## Disappearing Nine Patch Blocks (6" finished)

4 needed for inner top blocks (B) plus 7 for the outer border blocks (B)

From background (tan): Cut at least 4 - 2 1/2" strips, no longer than 20" each. Also needed: 2 - 6 1/2" plain blocks (C)

From outer border fabric (darkest brown): Cut at least 5 - 2 1/2" strips, no longer than 20" each. Use the rest of the fabric to cut outer border strips and squares.

From tan: Cut 6 - 7 1/2" setting blocks (D)

From darker gold: Cut 4 - 5 1/2" x 9 1/2" corner rectangles (E)

**Tip:** Unless you are cutting longer border strips, use the width of the fabric to cut sashing and patches from your fabric yardage. Always cut the longest and largest patches first.

# Sashing: (1 1/2" finished)

From background (tan): Cut 40 - 6 1/2" x 2" sashing strips

From gold: cut 24 - 2" squares for sash intersection squares

# Borders

Green inner border – 2" wide finished

Darkest brown outer border – 6" wide finished

From green: Cut 2 - 2 1/2" x 34 1/2" side border strips
Cut 2 - 2 1/2" x 38 1/2" top/bottom border strips

From darkest brown: Cut 3 - 6 1/2" x 32 1/2" border strips
Cut 2 - 6 1/2" x 13 1/2" border strips and
2 - 6 1/2" corner squares

## Backing, Batting and Binding

See General Instructions on pages 36-38.

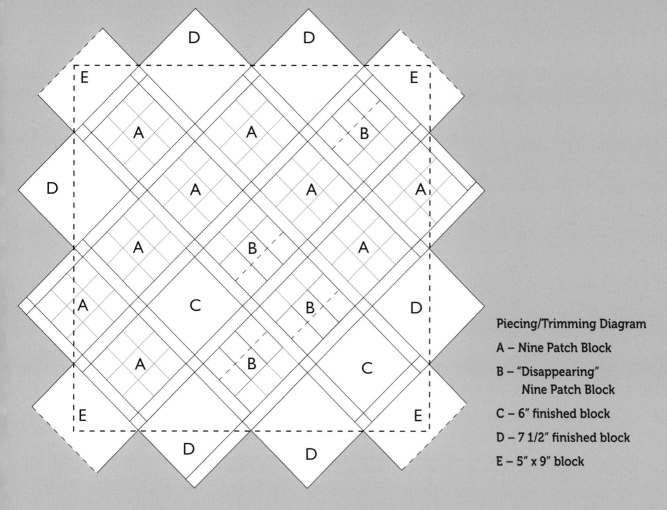

**Piecing/Trimming Diagram**

A – Nine Patch Block

B – "Disappearing" Nine Patch Block

C – 6" finished block

D – 7 1/2" finished block

E – 5" x 9" block

# Block Assembly

Traditional Nine Patches (6" finished):

1. Choose 3 - 2 1/2" strips and stitch together vertically; press.

2. Press, then cut 2 1/2" wedges from the sewn units. Stack in a pile.

3. Continue this process until you have at least 10-15 different piles of strip-pieced wedges to choose from. You may want to piece an occasional 'traditional' shaded block, like the mini-Nine patches in Framed Nine Patch (dark/light/dark, light/dark/light, dark/light/dark). In general, try to keep contrasting shades to a minimum. (See the quilt photo on page 106 for ideas.)

4. Make 9 blocks total.

## Disappearing Nine Patches (6" finished)

1. **Inner Quilt:** Make 4 blocks, using the same fabric scraps, process and stitching method as the traditional Nine Patches, but substituting background fabric (tan) for scrap strips used in the middle and/or bottom rows of the Nine Patch block. For at least one of these blocks, use all background fabrics for a bottom row and most of the middle row; however, stitch the similar-fabric strips together, just as if they'd been varying ones.

2. **Outer Border:** Make 7 blocks, using the same fabric scraps, process and stitching method as background Disappearing Nine Patch – but substitute outer border fabric (darkest brown) for the background.

**Tip:** In this quilt, the overall effect is far more important than individual blocks. Give yourself permission to experiment with unusual fabric and color combinations, then repeat those fabrics elsewhere in the quilt, for continuity.

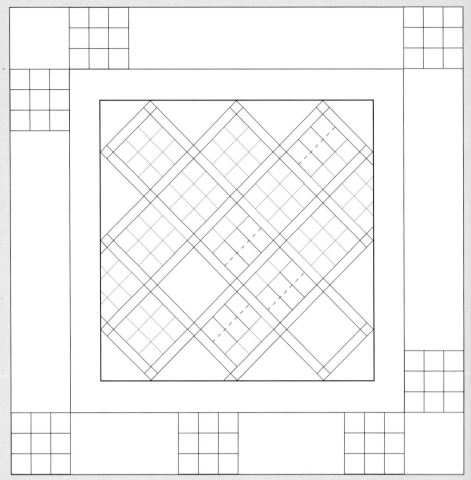

Assembly Diagram

# Quilt Assembly

## STITCHING AND TRIMMING THE TOP

(Refer to the Piecing/Trimming Diagram on page 109 and the quilt photo on page 106.)

1. Lay out the Traditional Nine Patch (A) and Disappearing Nine Patch (background) blocks (B), filling in with C, D and E blocks. Each block should be sashed with background (tan) on at least 2 sides, plus intersection squares.

2. Stitch sashing and intersection strips together in the sashing rows, then press and lay them back in place.

3. Join block rows together, adding sashed strips if they're needed to complete the block row. (Case in point: top left corner.)

4. Double-check. Does everything follow the general style of the Piecing/Trimming Diagram? Is the top pressed smooth on both front and back?

5. Using the dashed trim lines as a guide, use your rotary cutter and a longer ruler to trim away the outer parts of the pieced quilt. **Note:** *Use the outer tips of the intersection squares for lining up and cutting evenly. You will not cut evenly through some of the Nine Patch squares, however – no worries.*

6. Discard the cut fabrics and pieced sections, or use them for another project.

# Adding Borders

1. Add a shorter green inner border strip to each side of the top; press.

2. Add the top and bottom border strips to the top to complete the inner border. Press again.

3. Lay out the outer border strips and Disappearing Nine Patch outer border blocks (B) around the top-in-progress, following the Assembly Diagram and the quilt photo, until you're pleased with the arrangement.

4. Start with the outer border sides. Join a B to a long 6 1/2" x 32 1/2" outer border strip; press. Stitch in place on the left side of the quilt.

5. For the right side, alternate the 2 - 6 1/2" x 13 1/2" strips with the middle and top pieced Nine Patches, as shown. Stitch, press, then stitch in place on the right hand side of the quilt.

6. Use the same process to join the remaining 6 1/2" x 32 1/2" strips on top and bottom with the pieced Nine Patches and the plain corner blocks. Press, then add the top and bottom border strips, taking care to match corners where needed.

7. Press the top one more time, taking special care to make the back as tidy as the top. *(You won't regret it.)* Nearly done!

# Finishing the Quilt

Layer with batting and backing; baste. Trace the diamond cable quilting pattern on the outer border, if you like, using chalk or a lighter-colored marking pencil. Tie or quilt as desired; outline quilt the Nine Patch squares, especially the "disappearing" ones, to heighten the overall effect (see General Instructions on page 38). Bind to finish the quilt.

**Tip:** Now you've gotten the hang of it, why not try a different combination of shades and effects with this design? A bright red sashing strip, for example, could "float" on top of the quilt, along with the intersection squares, if you used a variety of medium darks and darks for the Nine Patch blocks. Different color combinations will change the piece's entire look, as well – floral pastels bordered with pinks and greens, latticed over with a pale/bright yellow "sunshine" sashing; a one-color celebration of purple, from lightest lavender to darkest purple; a Southwest combination of teal, brown and peach.

# MONEYBAGS

Here's a chance to make your own financial statement. Chinese Coins, a popular old pieced design, is interpreted in string-pieced fashion. (Add a large strip of gold if you're protesting the "Gold Standard" – or a bright green if it's an over-generous national Subsidy Plan!) Arrowhead-look piecing in each outer corner accents the sashed strips. Got any small cloth bags? Stitch one on the back of your quilt for your own personal "moneybag" – and stash a paper journal about your quilt inside.

## HOW TO MAKE MONEYBAGS

**FINISHED QUILT SIZE: 28" X 37 1/2"**

The pictured quilt takes the color cue of the dollar bill print used for the sashing – grayed blues and greens – and adds gold, silver and a touch of peach as an accent.

**Tip:** Having trouble deciding on fabrics for this quilt? Separate your prints by color, then try limiting the quilt to two colors, plus one or two colors as accents. (Black, white and even brown can act as neutrals.) Which pile should you choose for a multi-colored print? Lay it down – step back 5 or 6 steps. Whatever color comes first to mind: that's the pile to sort it into.

## FABRIC REQUIREMENTS

Assorted fabric scraps (string-pieced sashes): 3/4 yard

Sashing print ("dollar bill" sashes): fat quarter (18" x 22")

Green (outer border and 'arrowhead' squares): 1/2 yard

Cream (inner border): 1/4 yard.

Darker blue and green ('arrowhead' squares) 1/8 yard each

Backing: 1 1/4 yards (cut 32" x 41" piece)
Note: if fabric is 40" wide.

Batting: 32" x 41" rectangle

Binding: 1/4 yard

← **MONEYBAGS,** 2009, made by Bonnie DeVries and Cindy Brick. *Try this Chinese Coins variation in Amish-toned solid reds, yellows and blues for a totally different look.*

Also needed: scrap paper to stitch the sashes on – typing paper will do, or use the old-time favorite: newsprint. *(But be careful. The latter can get you – and your fabric – inky.)*

## CUTTING REQUIREMENTS
## SASHES

**String-Pieced Sashes** (5 needed)

Your fabric scraps should be in various-width strips ("strings").

Cut 5 - 5" x 21 1/2" paper rectangles from scrap paper.

**Plain Sashes** - "dollar bill" print (6 needed)

Cut 6 - 2 1/2" x 20 1/2" strips

## BORDERS

**From green:** Cut 2 - 1 1/2" x 20 1/2" inner border strips
Cut 2 - 1 1/2" x 32" inner border strips

**From cream:** Cut 2 - 3 1/2" x 16 1/2" outer border strips
Cut 2 - 3 1/2" x 26" outer border strips

Cut 4 - 4" squares – cut in half diagonally for 8 C triangles

**From each of darker blue and darker green:**
Cut 4 - 4" squares – cut in half diagonally for 8 C triangles

## Backing, Batting and Binding

See General Instructions on pages 36-38.

# Quilt Assembly
## STITCHING THE TOP

1. **String Piecing the Sashes:** Start in the middle of a paper rectangle – put a fabric scrap flat, then angle another scrap on top, right sides together. Stitch along the angled scrap. Trim away extra fabric, flip back and press. Continue stitching, changing angles now and then, until the rectangle is completely filled. Press one more time, then cut a 4" x 20 1/2" pieced sash. Make 4 more, for a total of 5. (Don't remove the paper until the top is completely pieced.)

2. Join the pieced sashes and regular sashes, alternating, and beginning/ending with a plain sash.

**Tip:** String Piecing Saves! This method is an amazing way to clear out your extra scraps – fast. Try string piecing squares, diamonds, circles – some quilters have even string-pieced the sashes that they used to enclose their string-pieced blocks! Random color and fabric choices are pretty...but make these scrap quilts even more effective by limiting yourself to just a few colors and a few accent colors. Or use just one color family for an extra-rich look. Piecing on fabric (and leaving it in) instead of paper makes a heavy but sturdy quilt.

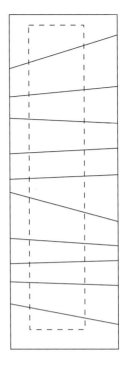

Cut section A from
pieced strips.

## ADDING BORDERS

1. Sew the side strips of the inner border on – then add the top and bottom strips.

2. **Corner blocks of outer border:**

Match and sew a dark blue C and cream C triangle together; make 4.

Repeat with a dark green C and cream C; make 4.

Repeat with a dark blue C and dark green C; make 4. Press all pieced triangle squares.

3. Lay out a corner's worth of pieced squares (1 each) to get the 'arrowhead' effect, using the quilt diagram for help. Keep it to look at while you:

*Join a dark blue/cream and dark green/cream square to either end of the long border strips.

*Do the same for either end of the short border strips.

*Add a dark green/dark blue square on each end of the longer strips, using the diagram to match for the 'arrowhead.' Press all pieced strips.

4. Lay out all outer border strips to double-check the 'arrowhead' corners.

5. Stitch the short borders on the sides of the quilt; match and add the longer pieced borders to the top and bottom to finish the top.

# Finishing the Quilt

1. Mark a quilting motif on each of the outer borders, if desired.

2. Gently pull away the bits and pieces of paper, using a tweezer for stubborn spots.

3. Layer the top with batting and backing; baste. Tie or quilt as you like (see General Instructions on page 38), then bind to finish the quilt.

**Tip:** Metallic fabrics are perfect for this quilt! So are embellishments like gold trim, iridescent and metallic ribbons, coin trim and buttons. Layer them back and forth on your pieced sashes, or use them to accent the borders.

**Assembly Diagram**

**A – pieced coins strip**

**B – sashing strip**

**C – pieced triangle squares**

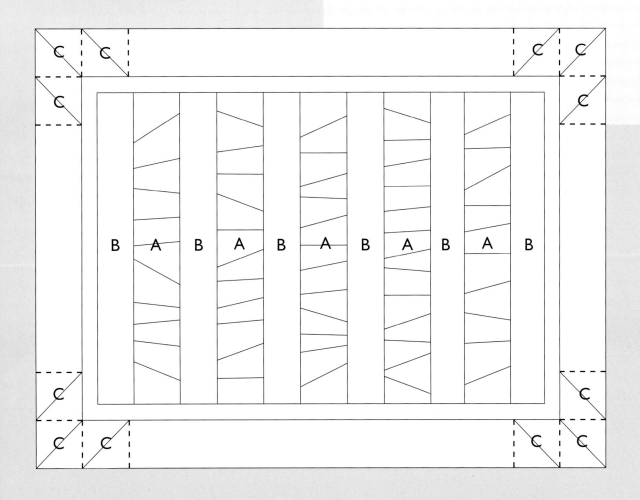

# TURKEY TRACKS

Pioneers headed west blessed their lucky stars when they saw wild turkey tracks – it meant a festive supper that night! Turkey meat, however tough and gamey, was a welcome change from the usual salt pork and dried beef. This design, a spiky variation on both Honeybee and the more rounded Oak Leaf, must have reminded its makers of birds' trails. It was rarely made, though, for a son's 21st birthday Freedom Quilt – the pattern was thought to inspire men to wander! ("Make tracks" was taken literally, apparently.) The clean lines and straightforward presentation are typical of a later 19th century appliqué quilt.

## HOW TO MAKE TURKEY TRACKS

FINISHED QUILT SIZE: 80" X 92"

### FABRIC REQUIREMENTS

California Gold (blocks): 1 yard

Red print (blocks): 1 3/4 yards (The quilt pictured uses the same fabric for binding, for a total of 2 3/4 yards)

Green print (blocks): 1 1/2 yards

Cream muslin (blocks and outer border): 7 1/8 yards

Backing: 8 1/2 yards (cut 3 - 32 1/2" x 96" lengths, and join vertically for backing)

Batting: 96" x 96" square

Binding: 1 yard (see note on red print, above)

### CUTTING REQUIREMENTS

**Border:** (4" finished)
**From white:** cut 2 - 4 1/2" x 72 1/2" top/bottom border strips *vertically* from yardage
Cut 2 - 4 1/2" x 92 1/2" side border strips *vertically* from yardage

**Blocks:** (12" finished – 21 Turkey Tracks appliquéd blocks, 21 plain alternating blocks, set 6 x 7 for a total of 42 blocks)

**From white:** Cut 42 – 12 ½" square blocks

**Note:** The curved-inner edge "pumpkin seed"-style center of this block can be stitched two ways: either with the red 'leaves' appliquéd around the California Gold circle (Method 1), or the California Gold curved center appliquéd on top of a red print circle (Method 2). Choose your method, then cut actual-sized patterns. Whichever method you choose, you also need A and B leaf patterns, also actual size. Trace each pattern directly on the fabric, using the template, then cut out, leaving enough space around the traced patch for an approximately 1/4" turn-under seam allowance.

*From red print:* (Cut binding strips first, if you've decided to use the same fabric)

Cut 4 A leaves, to use on each block center (if Method 1) x 21 blocks = 84 A leaves total  **OR**
Cut 21 block centers (if Method 2)
Also, cut 4 B leaves for each block (1 in each corner) x 21 blocks = 84 B leaves total

*From green print:*
Cut 8 A leaves for each block (2 per corner) x 21 blocks = 168 B leaves total

*From California Gold:*
Cut 21 block circles (if Method 1)  **OR**
Cut 21 curved-edge center pattern (if Method 2)

**TURKEY TRACKS**, *c.1885, collection of Rocky Mountain Quilt Museum*

Turkey
Tracks
Block
12" finished

## Backing, Batting and Binding

See General Instructions on pages 36-38.

# Block Assembly

### TURKEY TRACKS BASIC BLOCK:

1. Set aside 21 of the plain blocks for later.

2. Take 1 of the remaining 21 blocks, and fold it in half vertically and horizontally, then press. Center and pin a circle, using the pressed foldlines; use either Method 1 or Method 2 to finish the appliquéd center circle.

3. Arrange a pair of green A leaves at each curved point of the California Gold edge; appliqué in place.

4. Center 1 large red B leaf in between the green A leaves; appliqué in place. Use the block diagram throughout for help in positioning the patches.

5. Your block is done! Press it gently, then appliqué 20 more blocks.

**Tip:** Turning under the appliqué patch seam allowances can be done while the patch is still loose *(thread basting)*; then the basted patch is pinned and appliquéd in place on the fabric background. *(traditional appliqué)* Another method pins the patch in place on the block, then the edges of the patch are scraped under with a needle, a bit at a time, as you stitch it in place on the block. (This method is called *needle-turn appliqué*.) Whichever method works best for you, the marked line can be used as a turn-under guide.

# Quilt Assembly
## STITCHING THE TOP

1. Lay out the Turkey Track and plain alternating blocks in a row of 7, beginning and ending with a plain block in the first row.

2. Lay out the second row of 7 blocks, beginning and ending with a Turkey Tracks block.

3. Alternate these rows for 6 rows total. Use the quilt diagram for help.

4. Join blocks in the rows, then join the rows together, taking care to match seams.

## ADDING BORDERS

1. Fold a top/bottom border strip in half vertically, then use the folded line to center it on the bottom edge of the appliquéd top. Pin, working back to each edge. Stitch in place. Fold, press, position and stitch the top border strip in place.

2. Use the same method to stitch on the side border strips. Take care throughout not to pull the strip tight while you're stitching each in place; this causes wrinkling and distortion. Just smooth lightly in place as you stitch.

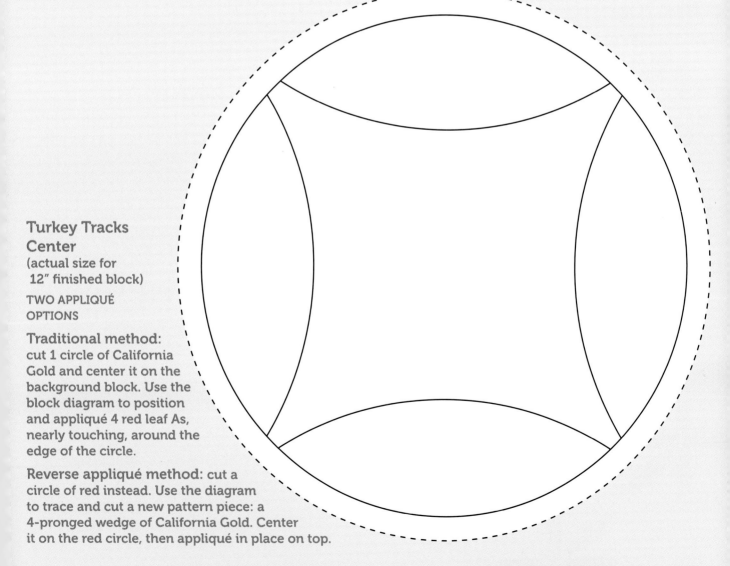

**Turkey Tracks Center**
(actual size for 12" finished block)

**TWO APPLIQUÉ OPTIONS**

**Traditional method:** cut 1 circle of California Gold and center it on the background block. Use the block diagram to position and appliqué 4 red leaf As, nearly touching, around the edge of the circle.

**Reverse appliqué method:** cut a circle of red instead. Use the diagram to trace and cut a new pattern piece: a 4-pronged wedge of California Gold. Center it on the red circle, then appliqué in place on top.

Leaf placement
(1/4 of the block/circle)

A: cut 8 green for
each block (2 for
each corner), cut
4 red for each block

B: cut 4 for each
block (1 in each
corner)

120

# Finishing the Quilt

Layer with batting and backing; baste. Tie or quilt as you like (see General Instructions on page 38), then bind to finish the quilt.

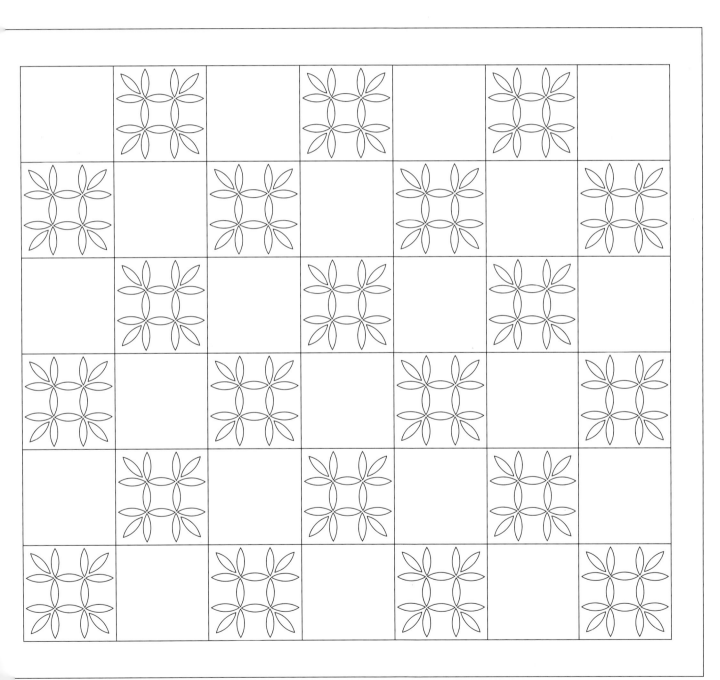

Assembly Diagram

CENTENNIAL TRIANGLES,
*c.1890, collection of the author*

# CENTENNIAL TRIANGLES

The last pattern in this book is one of the West's most popular scrap quilts...because it was so adaptable! Triangles march past, row by row, in varied scraps, colors and shades. Sometimes they were made with just two colors – a favorite method of redwork quilters. (See the Girls of the Golden West – Redwork Style on page 48 for more.) Sometimes each triangle was a different fabric. (See Charm Quilts below.) Many times, the quilter used whatever scraps she had, carefully cutting triangles and stashing them in a basket or box until she had enough to make a quilt. Often the fabrics ranged over several decades. Even today, your fabric scrap bag, like mine, may contain feedsacks from your grandma's time, subtle pindots and tiny 80s hearts from Mom...and batiks and paisleys from now. Be sure to include some reproduction prints as well, as a thank you to the pioneer quilters who first made this versatile quilt.

## HOW TO MAKE CENTENNIAL TRIANGLES

**FINISHED QUILT SIZE:** *WHAT DO YOU NEED?*

Some possibilities are given below: (assuming a 3" finished size triangle square)

**Nap/snuggle size:** 69" x 69" (23 rows of 23 pieced triangle squares: 529 squares total)

**Twin size:** 72" x 84"   (24 rows of 28 pieced triangle squares: 672 squares total)

**Queen size:** 84" x 96"   (28 rows of 32 pieced triangle squares: 896 squares total)

**King size:** 90" x 102"   (30 rows of 34 pieced triangle squares: 1020 squares total)

Or: measure your bed vertically and horizontally, including top and halfway down each side. Divide those measurements by the block size you choose (see below) to figure how many rows across and down of pieced triangle squares you need.

### Triangle Pattern Size:
*The patterns in this book often use a 1" finished or 2" finished pieced triangle square block. Any leftovers from those projects can be used in this quilt, as well! A slightly larger block – 3" finished – will let you make faster progress. The sample quilt sizes in this pattern are based on 3" finished triangle square blocks, but can be easily adapted to use the smaller squares.*

### FABRIC REQUIREMENTS
*Assorted light and dark fabric scraps (blocks):*

Snuggle quilt: 6 yards

Twin size: 8 yards

Queen size: 10 yards

King size: 11 1/2 yards

*Backing:* How big will your quilt be? Add 4" to the finished measurements, then decide how many panels you need to cut to join for the quilt backing. Use the **General Instructions** on pages 31-32 to help you figure yardage.

*Batting:* Add 4" to the finished quilt measurements – that's the size of your batting

*Binding:* 1/2 yard for a nap-sized quilt. For the other sizes, figure 1 yard. (You will have leftovers with some.)

**Assembly Diagram**

*Triangle Charm top detail, c.1890. Hundreds of different fabrics, dating from c.1860 – 1890, make up the triangles in this quilt.*

# Quilt Assembly

## STITCHING THE TOP

1. Lay out your triangle square blocks in rows. (One good way to do this: throw all the blocks into a paper sack, then pull them out randomly and put them down. Don't move any blocks because they clash with each other. Yet.)

2. Step back at least 5 paces. Take a good hard look. Are your colors evenly scattered across the face of the top? Break up any color 'clumps,' moving blocks around as needed. Are all the lights facing the same direction? Darks?

3. Walk away for at least an hour. (Preferably overnight.) Look again. Make any more changes needed.

4. Stitch the triangle square blocks together by rows, pressing each as you finish. Join the rows. Press your finished top. (Borders may be added, if desired – you need 2 yards for a thin border, and 4 yards for a thicker border.)

# CUTTING AND ASSEMBLY

## Blocks

**Triangle Pieced Squares** (3" finished size):

1. Cut a 4" square from a fabric scrap. Cut that square diagonally for two triangles. Sort triangles in piles of lights and darks. (If your planned triangle square is smaller or larger, visit "Triangle Rules" on page 45 for cutting help.)

2. Grab a triangle out of the 'lights' pile, preferably without looking. Grab another from the 'darks' pile, and match the two. Stitch and press.

3. Repeat- over and over and over!

# Backing, Batting and Binding

See General Instructions on pages 36-38.

# Finishing the Quilt

Layer with batting and backing; baste. Tie or quilt as you like (see General Instructions on page 38); old-time quilters often followed the diagonal lines of the triangles in an allover pattern. Bind to finish the quilt.

# Charmed, I'm Sure

Charm quilts played an important part in 19th century scrap quilting – especially for young unmarried girls. This type of quilt was simple in its execution: the same basic shape – square, rectangle, diamond, hexagon, triangle, etc. – was used to cut quilt patches from a wide variety of fabrics. Then the shapes were joined together without sashing for an allover design of scrap fabrics.

The charm quilt's simplicity was complicated by another rule: none of the fabrics could be the same. This meant haunting the local dry goods store for the latest prints. Trading with friends. Getting pieces from family members – or even the boyfriend's new tie, shirt or vest! Pretending to be salesmen, girls would even contact fabric manufacturers and request samples of the newest lines. (The manufacturers eventually realized the deceit and either required proof, or sent samples too small to be cut.) The charm quilt gained another name from this subterfuge, one it shared with Crazy quilts: "beggar's patchwork."

Why did young girls go to all this trouble? Because the charm quilt, besides its beauty, was also thought to be a sure cure for singleness. Piece 999 different fabric patches together, add a thousandth patch… and get married!

*Civil War Sampler, c.1855, cut for use on a four-poster bed. Great-Grandmother Opperman is thought to have made this piece as a wedding gift, with the help of the bride's family and friends. Many different 'hands' appear in the blocks' work – they're joined with an unusual (for this period, anyway) "quilt-as-you-go" technique. Many a quilt in this style, which dated back into the 18th century, went west in emigrants' wagons. Collection of Janice Fisher.*

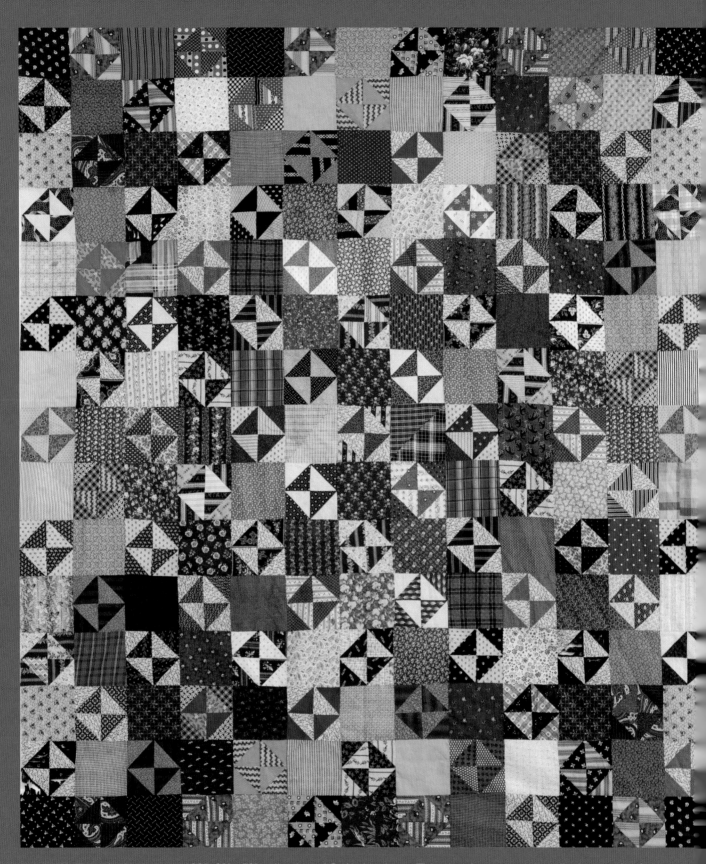

*Dutch Triangles Variation, c.1885, 82" x 72", collection of Cathy Litwinow. This triangle pattern is literally thousands of years old, and has been used in everything from ceramics to floor rugs. Tile floors in the pattern have been pictured in Dutch interiors by early painters like Vermeer. The golden prints in this pretty scrap top? That's just California Gold, doing its job.*

Urbancowgirl.com, Jean Ray Laury, 2000. Want to be a Cowgirl? Jean's version reminds us that the Internet is one way to get there...whether or not you live in the Golden West. Photo by EZ Smith.

# SOURCES

Bond, Dorothy. *Crazy Quilt Stitches* (self-published: Cottage Grove, OR, 1981).

Brackman, Barbara. *Encyclopedia of Pieced Quilt Patterns* (American Quilter's Society: Paducah, KY, 1993). *Encyclopedia of Appliqué* (Howell Press: Charlottesville, VA, 1993).

Brick, Cindy. *Crazy Quilts: History, Information, Projects* (Voyageur Press: Menasha, WI, 2008). *A Stitcher's Language of Flowers* (Brickworks Press: Castle Rock, CO, 2005).

Burnham, Tom. *The Dictionary of Misinformation* (Perennial Library/ Harper & Row, Publishers: New York, NY, 1975).

Butruille, Susan. *Women's Voices from the Mother Lode: Tales from the California Gold Rush* (Tamarack Books: Boise, ID, 2003).

Chartier, JoAnn and Enss, Chris. *With Great Hope: Women of the California Gold Rush* (TwoDot/Falcon Publishing: San Ramon, CA, 2000).

Connell, Evan S. *Son of the Morning Star: Custer and the Little Bighorn* (Harper Perennial: New York, NY, 1991).

Groushko, Mike. *Treasure: Lost, Found & Undiscovered* (Shooting Star Press: New York, NY, 1990).

Hall, W.C. and Jameson, Wendell E. *Buried Treasures of the American Southwest* (National Book Network: Lanham, MD, 1989).

Holmes, Kenneth. (editor) *Covered Wagon Women: Vol. 1 Diaries and Letters from the Western Trail, 1840-49* (Bison Books: Lincoln, NE, 1995). *Other volumes from this series, which was printed 1995-2000, were also used.*

Horn, Jeanne. *Hidden Treasure: How and Where to Find It* (Arco Publishing Co: New York, NY, 1962).

Kazin, Michael. *A Godly Hero: The Life of William Jennings Bryan* (Anchor/ Random House: New York, NY, 2007).

Laury, Jean Ray and the California Heritage Quilt Project. *Ho for California!: Pioneer Women and Their Quilts* (EP Dutton: New York, NY, 1990).

Kinder, Gary. *Ship of Gold in the Deep Blue Sea* (Vintage/Random House Books: New York, NY, 1998.)

Levy, Jo Ann. *They Saw the Elephant: Women in the California Gold Rush* (University of Oklahoma Press: Norman, OK, 1992).

Meacham, Jon. *American Lion: Andrew Jackson in the White House* (Random House: New York, NY, 2008).

Mihm, Stephen. *A Nation of Counterfeiters: Capitalists, Con Men, and The Making of the United States* (Harvard University Press: Cambridge, MA, 2007).

Murphy, Claire. *Gold Rush Women* (Alaska Northwest Books: Anchorage, AK, 2003).

Rourke, Constance. *Troupers of the Gold Coast: or The Rise of Lotta Crabtree* (Harcourt, Brace & Co: New York, NY, 1928).

Schroeder, Alice. *The Snowball: Warren Buffett and the Business of Life* (Bantam Dell/Random House: New York, NY, 2008).

Von Mueller, Karl. *Treasure Hunter's Manual #6 & #7* (Ram Books: Dallas, TX, 1979).

Yalom, Marilyn and Reid. *The American Resting Place: 400 Years of History Through Our Cemeteries and Burial Grounds* (Houghton Mifflin Harcourt: New York, NY, 2008).

Zanjani, Sally. *A Mine of Her Own: Women Prospectors in the American West 1850-1950* (Bison Books: Lincoln, NE, 2000).

Harison's Yellow Roses are available from Split Mountain Garden Center in Jensen, UT, or mail order from High Country Roses: P.O. Box 148, Jensen, UT 84035, 1-800-552-2082 (toll-free) roses@easilink.com *www.highcountryroses.com*